are you happy?

are you happy?

THE PSYCHOLOGIST'S BOOK OF
HAPPINESS TESTS

+ + +

Louis Janda, Ph.D.

A Perigee Book

A Perigee Book
Published by the Penguin Group
Penguin Group (USA) Inc.
375 Hudson Street, New York, New York 10014, USA
Penguin Group (Canada), 10 Alcorn Avenue, Toronto, Ontario M4V 3B2, Canada
(a division of Pearson Penguin Canada Inc.)
Penguin Books Ltd., 80 Strand, London WC2R 0RL, England
Penguin Group Ireland, 25 St. Stephen's Green, Dublin 2, Ireland (a division of Penguin Books Ltd.)
Penguin Group (Australia), 250 Camberwell Road, Camberwell, Victoria 3124, Australia
(a division of Pearson Australia Group Pty. Ltd.)
Penguin Books India Pvt. Ltd., 11 Community Centre, Panchsheel Park, New Delhi – 110 017, India
Penguin Group (NZ), cnr. Airborne and Rosedale Roads, Albany, Auckland 1310, New Zealand
(a division of Pearson New Zealand Ltd.)
Penguin Books (South Africa) (Pty.) Ltd., 24 Sturdee Avenue, Rosebank, Johannesburg 2196,
South Africa
Penguin Books Ltd., Registered Offices: 80 Strand, London WC2R 0RL, England

PRINTING HISTORY
Perigee trade paperback edition / December 2004

This book has been cataloged by the Library of Congress
Janda, Louis H.
    Are you happy? : 24 self-tests to assess your happiness / Louis Janda.—1st Perigee pbk. ed.
    p. cm.
    "A Perigee book."
    ISBN 0-399-53034-7
    1. Happiness—Testing. 2. Self-report inventories. I. Title
    BF575.H27J37 2004
    646.7'0028'7—dc22

PRINTED IN THE UNITED STATES OF AMERICA   2004050503

10 9 8 7 6 5 4 3 2 1

for my wife, tina, who makes it possible for me
to experience much happiness

contents

introduction

We psychologists are a pessimistic and gloomy lot. Going back more than a hundred years to Sigmund Freud and his theory of psychoanalysis, the focus of our discipline has always been on what is wrong with people, their problems and their pathologies. And to a large extent, this focus has paid rich dividends. We have made great strides in understanding the causes of many psychological disorders and considerable progress in treating these conditions, although we have a long way to go. But this emphasis on the negative has had broader implications than merely focusing our attention on disorders—it has led to rather dreary assumptions about human nature. Freud argued that our most basic needs were to satisfy our sexual and aggressive impulses and if we somehow managed to lead a satisfying life, a life in which we were helpful and kind to others, a life in which we could take pleasure, it was a result of our attempts to compensate for our darker impulses. People are not good for the sake of goodness, this view suggests; they are only good so they can deny their baneful impulses.

During the late 1960s and early 1970s psychology experienced something of a respite, however brief, from this dark view of human nature. These were the years in which the humanistic theorists, people such as Carl Rogers and Abraham Maslow, were generating a great deal of excitement. These psychologists objected to the notion that to become kind, loving, and happy people, we had to learn to keep our base impulses under control. They believed that we have an innate drive to develop in a positive direction, or in Maslow's words, to become "self-actualized." These humanistic views were the mirror image of mainstream theory. While Freud believed it was the role of society to place controls on people so their aggressive and destructive impulses would not make it to the surface, Rogers and Maslow argued that, were it not for society's strictures, people would naturally proceed along the path that led to self-actualization. Despite this positive view of human nature, the humanistic theorists did not place much stock in happiness. They were more interested in qualities such as authenticity, integrity, and a persistent striving to reach one's full potential. Happiness, if considered at all, was viewed as a somewhat frivolous and not especially important by-product of deeper and supposedly more meaningful characteristics.

This brief flowering of humanistic psychology soon wilted as empirical evidence found that the movement's techniques failed to deliver all that they had promised. Mainstream psychology reverted to its focus on pathologies and disorders and its tendency to denigrate admirable, even joyful human qualities as resulting from some deep, dark, inner conflict. Indeed, the *Diagnostic and Statistical Manual* (known simply as *DSM-IV* to those in the profession), the single most influential book in psychiatry and clinical psychology, describes the qualities of affiliation, anticipation, humor, and even altruism as defense mechanisms. It must seem very odd to the layperson that so many mental health professionals will speculate on what is wrong with a person who is altruistic. This seems odd to a growing number of psychologists as well.

Because happiness is a central concern for so many people, one would think that research psychologists would have jumped on this topic right from the start. But it was not until well into the second half of the twentieth century that researchers paid much attention to the emotion that we are all hoping to experience. In 1967 Warner Wilson published one of the first review articles on happiness in which he summarized what psychology knew about this topic; and although many of his conclusions turned out to be wrong, his article did have the effect of stimulating interest in the area. The following two decades saw an increase in the number of scientific journal articles devoted to this topic, and in 1999, the *Journal of Happiness Studies* was founded. About that time Martin Seligman was elected president of the American Psychological Association. During his tenure, he forcefully argued that psychology should shift its focus from what is wrong with people to what is right with them, from their weaknesses to their strengths, from their limitations to their capacity to experience a full range of joyful, satisfying emotions. Positive psychology finally found a place in the discipline as we moved into the twenty-first century.

Psychologists have learned a great deal about happiness over the past decade, but perhaps the most important thing we have learned is that it is possible to address a person's feelings of happiness directly and, for those who are not as happy as they would like to be, to apply techniques to enhance their positive experiences. This is important because, historically, philosophers and psychologists alike believed that happiness is little more than a fortuitous by-product of a life well lived. So if we work hard, get a good education, perform well on our job, and treat our family and friends with love and kindness, we have a chance to be happy.

But the truth of the matter is that there are lots of people who do all these things and still do not experience much happiness. It is the case that these people's ability to feel happy may be limited by their genetic predisposition, but we also have discovered techniques that can increase their capacity to experience joy and happiness.

It is important to keep in mind that positive psychologists are ultimately concerned with long-term happiness. The techniques they have to offer do not promise any shortcuts, because shortcuts simply do not work. Calling in sick for a day on the golf course, indulging in sex or drugs, or engaging in any number of other momentarily pleasurable activities may produce a brief spike in happiness, but they are merely distractions and have the potential to actually reduce our happiness over the long run. That short-term pleasure does not lead to lasting happiness was vividly demonstrated by British researchers who studied 191 people who won a large amount of money on soccer pools. As a group, they were slightly happier than nonwinners, but a significant number of these people reported that their lives were worse after winning. They had quit their jobs and moved to nicer neighborhoods, thus losing many old friends and acquaintances. And their family relationships deteriorated as a result of quarrels over money. I have to confess, though, that despite this research I still would not throw away a winning lottery ticket.

Positive psychologists agree that we must have a solid foundation on which to build happiness. I would guess that most of you reading this book already have this foundation. You have worked hard; you have done your best to live your life well. For those of you who fall into this category your task is relatively simple, though it may not be easy. Use the tests in this book to identify your strengths and build on them. Identify your weaknesses and correct them. I suspect that Chapter 14, which discusses positive mood states, will be especially useful for you.

A few of you will have a lot more work to do. If you have made it a habit to chose momentary pleasures over working toward long-term goals, you need to work on your foundation. While the idea of changing the structure of your life can be daunting, it can also be highly satisfying, so do not allow yourself to become discouraged along the way. Truly, it is never too late to change—so begin today, do not put it off. Chapter 9, which focuses on goals, is one that you should pay close attention to.

+ about the tests in this book

I selected the tests that appear in this book because they reflect issues that have been investigated by positive psychologists. The link between each one of these topics and happiness has been explored, sometimes, as you will discover, with surprising results. My goal in selecting each of the quizzes is to help readers increase their understanding of what they need to do to feel happier. I hope you will let me know how successful I have been with my choices.

Please keep two thoughts in mind as you go through the book. First, these tests are not intended to be diagnostic instruments. Consequently, if you should receive a very low score on the Friendships Tests (Chapter 1), for instance, it does not necessarily mean that you have serious problems with your interpersonal relationships. Although it probably is the case that improving the quality of your friendships could help you feel happier, the tests were not designed to detect pathology and you should never interpret a low score as an indicator of a serious problem. You should think of the tests as guides that will provide you with food for thought. They may help you be a little more objective about your life, but they cannot reveal anything about you that you do not already know. They are self-report instruments, meaning you are the one doing the reporting. Should you feel distressed about any of the results, it might be a good idea for you to discuss your feelings with a mental health professional.

The second caveat is that the order in which I have presented the tests does not reflect their relative importance. Because the field of positive psychology is so new, we have much to learn about the relative importance of the components of happiness and even more to learn about their interrelationships. These questions can be quite tricky. For example, I believe that, for most people, having good relationships with family and friends is essential to happiness, but having good relationships is related to a number of other factors, such as optimism, altruism, and emotional stability. Because we are only beginning to understand how these qualities fit together, there are no hard-and-fast rules to guide the person who might receive low scores on all of these tests. It may be that a person who improves his or her relationships will become more altruistic or emotionally stable. Or it may be that one must become emotionally stable and altruistic before one can hope to have better relationships. I suspect that it can work both ways and that you, the reader, are the best judge of deciding the approach for you. Again, do not hesitate to seek professional help if you have trouble getting started with your plans to change.

+ a few words about norms

Following each test are instructions that allow you to express your results in terms of a percentile score—a concept you probably remember from all those achievement tests you took during your school years. Percentiles allow you to compare your score to the scores of a larger group of people. A percentile score of 85, for instance, means that your score is higher than 85 percent of the people who took the test. I have used five percentile levels to help you interpret your results: 15, 30, 50, 70, and 85. This scale allows you to determine how far above or below average you have scored. The percentile scores for these tests are based on rather small samples so, once again, I want to remind you not to become unduly concerned about a very low score. These scores should serve only as rough guidelines to help you begin your effort to become a happier person.

Okay, the time has come. You can take the tests in the order in which they appear, but it is not essential to do so. Feel free to skip around, depending on your own interests and needs. The process of self-discovery can be enjoyable and rewarding, and I hope you find that this is true for you. Above all else, I hope this book will help you become a happier person.

are you happy?

PART ONE

relationships

+ + +

do your friendships make you happy?

The following phrases describe people's behaviors, attitudes, and feelings. Indicate the extent to which you agree that the statement describes you.

1. When I am around others, I feel like I am part of the crowd.

1	2	3	4	5
strongly disagree	disagree	neither agree nor disagree	agree	strongly agree

2. When I have a problem, there is no one I can turn to.

1	2	3	4	5
strongly disagree	disagree	neither agree nor disagree	agree	strongly agree

3. It is easy to be myself when I am with my friends.

1	2	3	4	5
strongly disagree	disagree	neither agree nor disagree	agree	strongly agree

4. I know many people who share my interests and values.

1	2	3	4	5
strongly disagree	disagree	neither agree nor disagree	agree	strongly agree

5. I don't know anyone with whom I can talk with freely.

1	2	3	4	5
strongly disagree	disagree	neither agree nor disagree	agree	strongly agree

6. When I am around someone I do not know, I introduce myself.

1	2	3	4	5
strongly disagree	disagree	neither agree nor disagree	agree	strongly agree

7. If a close friend moved away, I would feel sad for a long time.

1	2	3	4	5
strongly disagree	disagree	neither agree nor disagree	agree	strongly agree

8. It is easy for me to talk to people I do not know well.

1	2	3	4	5
strongly disagree	disagree	neither agree nor disagree	agree	strongly agree

9. I feel isolated much of the time.

1	2	3	4	5
strongly disagree	disagree	neither agree nor disagree	agree	strongly agree

10. I often feel left out.

1	2	3	4	5
strongly disagree	disagree	neither agree nor disagree	agree	strongly agree

11. I often feel close to other people.

1	2	3	4	5
strongly disagree	disagree	neither agree nor disagree	agree	strongly agree

12. I have friends who really understand me.

1	2	3	4	5
strongly disagree	disagree	neither agree nor disagree	agree	strongly agree

13. My friends often confide in me about their personal problems.

1	2	3	4	5
strongly disagree	disagree	neither agree nor disagree	agree	strongly agree

14. I enjoy it when others share ideas that are different from my own.

1	2	3	4	5
strongly disagree	disagree	neither agree nor disagree	agree	strongly agree

15. When I make a promise to a friend, I keep it.

1	2	3	4	5
strongly disagree	disagree	neither agree nor disagree	agree	strongly agree

16. I am quick to offer praise to the people I work with.

1	2	3	4	5
strongly disagree	disagree	neither agree nor disagree	agree	strongly agree

17. I am not sure that anyone knows me really well.

1	2	3	4	5
strongly disagree	disagree	neither agree nor disagree	agree	strongly agree

18. I often feel lonely even when I am with other people.

1	2	3	4	5
strongly disagree	disagree	neither agree nor disagree	agree	strongly agree

19. When I feel the need, it is easy for me to find companionship.

1	2	3	4	5
strongly disagree	disagree	neither agree nor disagree	agree	strongly agree

20. I would rather spend time with friends than read or watch television.

1	2	3	4	5
strongly disagree	disagree	neither agree nor disagree	agree	strongly agree

+ scoring

The first step is to reverse score items 2, 5, 9, 10, 17, and 18.
For these items, if you circled 5, change it to a 1, a 4 becomes a
2, a 3 remains a 3, a 2 becomes a 4, and a 1 becomes a 5.

This test consists of two scales, a Connectedness Scale and a
Friendliness Scale. To find your connectedness score, add your
points for items 1, 2, 4, 9, 10, 11, 12, 17, 18, and 19. To find
your friendliness score, add your points for items 3, 5, 6, 7, 8,
13, 14, 15, 16, and 20. High scores on these scales indicate a
high level of connectedness, friendliness, and ease in interacting
with others.

CONNECTEDNESS SCORE	FRIENDLINESS SCORE	PERCENTILE
42	40	85
38	36	70
33	31	50
28	26	30
24	22	15

+ about the friendships test

Happy people see themselves as having good relationships
with others, and they spend more time socializing with friends
than their unhappy counterparts. If you received a low score on
the Connectedness Test, there is a good chance you could be happier if you improved your ability to connect with other people.
Your score on the Friendliness Test provides clues to the approach
that would work best to accomplish this goal.

A majority of people who have low scores on the Connectedness Test also have low scores on the Friendliness Test. These people would like to have better social relationships, but they lack the necessary skills. They tend to be shy, introverted, and nonassertive people who are lacking in self-confidence. People who have these qualities often feel powerless to do anything to change their lives, but decades of research have shown that it is possible to do so. The skills needed to make new friends and to maintain close relationships can be learned, though it takes effort and persistence.

A good place to begin is with the image you project to others. In his research dealing with friendliness, psychologist John Reisman of DePaul University found that lonely people often knew the right things to say to other people but they were not very good at saying them.

A woman I once saw in therapy provides a good example of this. Ellen came to therapy five years after her divorce, because she was painfully lonely. She had not dated at all since her divorce, despite being above average in attractiveness and despite having a job where she regularly interacted with others. Ellen suffered from poor self-esteem and her feelings caused her to erect a barrier around herself. When she would meet someone for the first time, her self-doubts would keep her from smiling, making eye contact, and engaging in all the little nonverbal behaviors that communicate our interest in and acceptance of others. The first task I assigned Ellen was simply to pretend that she was a friendly, outgoing person. When she went to the grocery store or to the shopping mall, she had to take advantage of opportunities to make eye contact with others and to smile warmly. To her surprise, she found that people began to react to her quite differently from the way they had in the past. Over the following weeks, she had a couple of conversations with others while waiting in line in stores, and she began to perceive the world as being a friendlier place.

Ellen did not understand how others perceived her. While she had assumed that her inability to make new friends represented some deficit in her, she was projecting an image of a person who did not want to be bothered, of a woman who was saying, "Don't you dare approach me." By making modest changes in her behavior, Ellen learned that other people did respond to her. Not everyone responded to her new image, but enough people did to provide her with the necessary confidence to go on to the next step.

Ellen's second assignment was to initiate conversations with others. When someone returned her smile while waiting for an elevator, for instance, her task was to say something simple such as, "How are you today?" or "It's a beautiful day today, isn't it?" Once again she discovered that while there were some sour people in the world, many others responded to her with warmth and kindness. After several weeks of practice, Ellen came to therapy one day with the insight that her behavior on her job probably came across as abrupt and distant. She worked on changing her demeanor and results quickly followed. She enjoyed having conversations with her clients, however brief, and she began to perceive her colleagues as friendlier as well. For the first time in years, Ellen discovered that she no longer dreaded Monday mornings.

Ellen's third assignment was to expand her activities. This was the hardest step for her because she felt self-conscious doing these things alone, but she did begin to attend community lectures and she registered for a class in photography at her community center. Her efforts paid off when she met two women with whom she became friends. Ellen continued to make progress; and although she never became an extrovert, she was able to connect with enough people to enrich her life and eliminate her feelings of isolation and loneliness.

I always worry that a brief case history, such as Ellen's, makes it sound as if it were easy to make the changes necessary to improve one's life. It is rarely easy, but it *is* possible. Ellen began with many strengths, but nonetheless she needed much encouragement to persevere with her efforts to change. The point is that with persistence and effort, and sometimes with the help of a competent therapist, it is possible to change. It is always possible to have a better, happier life, as long as one does not give up.

There are a few people who have low scores on the Connectedness Test but who have high scores on the Friendliness Test. These people describe themselves as friendly and outgoing but, nonetheless, they feel lonely and isolated. Although they do not seem to have any problems initiating conversations and talking to others, they do not seem to be able to connect in any meaningful way. If this describes you, you might need the assistance of a family member or close friend to help you take a close look at yourself. You may be confusing talkativeness with friendliness.

Ed was one of these people. He had no difficulty in initiating conversations with others, but his favorite topics were his own accomplishments and *his* view on any conceivable subject. He rarely listened to what others had to say beyond waiting for an opening to shift the focus of conversation to himself. Ed could not understand why he had so few friends given his outgoing nature, but he finally found the courage to take a close look at himself after his wife left him because she could not tolerate his constant criticism. He was stunned to learn that he was generally perceived to be a know-it-all braggart; but with the help of a sensitive social worker, he was able to learn not only to let others talk about themselves but to encourage them to do so. He had to learn to bite his tongue, to keep himself from telling others the "right way" to handle various situations. Over time he discovered that as he showed more interest in others, they began to show more interest in him. And his wife, encouraged by his attempts to change, agreed to try a reconciliation. As with Ellen, the changes Ed made were not easy for him, but his efforts paid rich dividends.

+ 2 +

are you satisfied with your romantic relationship?

The following phrases describe people's behaviors, attitudes, and feelings. Indicate the extent to which you agree that the statement describes you.

1. I can't imagine life without my partner.

1	2	3	4	5
strongly disagree	disagree	neither agree nor disagree	agree	strongly agree

2. When something exciting happens to me, the first thing I want to do is to tell my partner about it.

1	2	3	4	5
strongly disagree	disagree	neither agree nor disagree	agree	strongly agree

3. My partner is very attractive to me.

1	2	3	4	5
strongly disagree	disagree	neither agree nor disagree	agree	strongly agree

4. I am proud when I introduce my partner to my friends and family.

1	2	3	4	5
strongly disagree	disagree	neither agree nor disagree	agree	strongly agree

5. Our relationship isn't as important to my partner as it is to me.

1	2	3	4	5
strongly disagree	disagree	neither agree nor disagree	agree	strongly agree

6. The frequency with which my partner and I have sex is just right for me.

1	2	3	4	5
strongly disagree	disagree	neither agree nor disagree	agree	strongly agree

7. The frequency with which my partner and I have arguments seems typical to me.

1	2	3	4	5
strongly disagree	disagree	neither agree nor disagree	agree	strongly agree

8. When my partner and I have an argument, we may say hurtful things that we later regret.

1	2	3	4	5
strongly disagree	disagree	neither agree nor disagree	agree	strongly agree

9. I wish it were easier for my partner to express affection.

1	2	3	4	5
strongly disagree	disagree	neither agree nor disagree	agree	strongly agree

10. I believe my partner tries as hard as I do to make our relationship successful.

1	2	3	4	5
strongly disagree	disagree	neither agree nor disagree	agree	strongly agree

11. I believe that my relationship will last forever.

1	2	3	4	5
strongly disagree	disagree	neither agree nor disagree	agree	strongly agree

12. I am easily excited when my partner caresses me.

1	2	3	4	5
strongly disagree	disagree	neither agree nor disagree	agree	strongly agree

13. I sometimes wonder what life would be like if I were with someone else.

1	2	3	4	5
strongly disagree	disagree	neither agree nor disagree	agree	strongly agree

14. My partner is able to comfort me when I am feeling bad.

1	2	3	4	5
strongly disagree	disagree	neither agree nor disagree	agree	strongly agree

15. It makes me feel good when my partner gives me compliments.

1	2	3	4	5
strongly disagree	disagree	neither agree nor disagree	agree	strongly agree

+ scoring

The first step is to reverse score items 5, 8, 9, and 13. For these items, if you circled 5, change it to a 1, a 4 becomes a 2, a 3 remains a 3, a 2 becomes a 4, and a 1 becomes a 5. After you have made these changes, add your points together for your total score on the Romantic Relationship Test. High scores indicate a high level of satisfaction with your romantic relationship.

ROMANTIC RELATIONSHIP SCORE	PERCENTILE
60	85
56	70
52	50
48	30
42	15

+ about the romantic relationship test

A happy romantic relationship can make all the difference in the world. A tough day at work, an unpaid bill, or a fussy child can seem to be nothing more than minor irritants if, at the end of the day, you feel joy while holding your partner in your arms as you fall asleep. If you received a score of 62 or higher on the Romantic Relationship Test, you are one of these fortunate people. If your score was closer to 42, you may want to examine your relationship closely and consider making some changes that could make it more satisfying.

As anyone who watches the afternoon talk shows knows, there are countless experts who believe they have the answer to what makes a relationship satisfying. One of the most widely respected of these experts in the professional community is Robert Sternberg of Yale University, who has conducted extensive research on the nature of love and relationships. Sternberg's work has resulted in what he calls a "triangular theory of love," which suggests that there are three components of love: intimacy, passion, and commitment. Several of the items in the Romantic Relationship Test reflect these dimensions. Items 2 and 4 reflect intimacy, for instance; items 3 and 12 measure passion; and items 1, 11, and 13 indicate your level of commitment. The happiest relationships are those in which a healthy dose of all three components are present, although it is possible for people to be satisfied with a relationship in which at least one of these components has faded. The most common example is couples in a long-term relationship in which passion is more of a pleasant memory than a current reality but who retain a strong sense of intimacy and commitment.

One of the most interesting findings of Sternberg's research is that the happiest couples are those who have "congruent" love triangles. This suggests that it is not the absolute strength of the components of love that matters most, but rather that your partner's feelings for you are similar to your feelings for your partner. We have all known couples like this. John and Sylvia, for instance, were quite happy together, although they never confided in each other very much. While they both had a strong commitment to their marriage and both enjoyed their regular, if infrequent, sexual encounters, they were both very private people who found it difficult to share their innermost feelings, even with each other. Had either of them married someone else, the odds are good they would have been accused of being cold and aloof. But because they had similar ideas about the role of intimacy in a relationship, they were quite happy with each other. If you circled mostly 4s and 5s on items 5, 6, 7, 9, and 10, you and your partner probably do have congruent love triangles.

Given that sexual incompatibility is consistently one of the most common reasons for divorce, differences in passion are most likely to lead to incongruent love triangles. This is tragic because with a little patience and understanding, most couples could learn to deal with this difference. Carl and Monica's relationship got off to a fast start. Carl wanted to have sex daily, and Monica was happy to participate even though she preferred a more leisurely schedule. But as the years passed, Carl's interest waned while Monica's stayed steady. After ten years of marriage, once a week was plenty for Carl, but this left Monica feeling deprived and unloved. She tried to take the initiative, but Carl withdrew; he told her he "just wasn't interested." And the more pressure Monica applied, the less interested Carl became. Before their fifteenth anniversary, Monica filed for divorce. She refused "to live like a nun."

Had Carl been more sensitive to his wife's feelings, he could

have strengthened his relationship rather than destroy it. Monica
wanted to feel loved and valued as much as she wanted release
from sexual tension. It was not critical that every physical encounter end in sexual intercourse, and Carl could have fulfilled
his wife's needs by holding her, caressing her, and pleasuring her
in a variety of ways. Selfish people rarely have happy relationships. And, as we will see shortly, perhaps Monica could have
helped her husband understand this.

Psychologist Robyn Dawes added an interesting perspective
to the importance of sex in marriage. He found that frequency
of sex was not related to happiness with the relationship. As we
have suggested, some couples may be happy as long as they have
sex on their anniversary, whereas others want it on a much more
regular basis. Dawes also found that the frequency of arguments
was not related to happiness with the relationship. Again, some
couples rarely exchange a harsh word, while others feel something is missing if they don't have a good argument every now
and then. But Dawes found that, taken together, frequency of sex
and frequency of arguments did predict the couple's happiness
with their marriage and that there appeared to be a critical ratio
of about three to one. Couples who had sex three times for every
argument were happier than those who fell below this ratio.

When researchers began to address the topic of romantic love
back in the late 1960s and early 1970s, one of the first discoveries (and perhaps the most disturbing to many people) is that
feelings of romantic love fade with time. Most everyone in a
solid long-term relationship is well aware of this, but many people commit to a partner because they believe their happiness is
intertwined with the intensity of their romantic love. Unfor-
tunately, when the feelings of romantic love begin to fade away
(about eighteen to thirty-six months for most people), many of

these men and women learn that they don't really like their partner and are miserable in their relationship. Couples in successful, happy, long-term relationships have feelings of liking, respect, and affection for their partner. These are the men and women who find themselves in the envious position of being married to their best friend.

Because romantic love fades with time, it is foolish to risk our long-term happiness on it. Men and women would be wise to ensure that they like and respect their partner before they make a commitment. Items 4 and 8 will provide a sense of whether these essential ingredients are a part of your relationship. The odds of finding happiness in a relationship in which the people do not like and respect each other are very slim.

If you feel unhappy in your romantic relationship, there is a good chance you can improve it, but it does take diligence and hard work. You must identify the ingredients you feel are missing, and you must communicate this in a loving, nonthreatening way to your partner. Let's return to Carl and Monica for a moment. Although it is tempting to see Carl as the bad guy for neglecting his wife's needs, it is possible that their marriage could have been saved had Monica approached her husband differently. Rather than becoming angry and questioning his virility when Carl rejected her advances, Monica may have been able to get what she wanted had she said something like, "Can you hold me and caress me. I want to feel your love."

My experience with counseling couples has taught me that even the most clear and loving communication will not save all relationships. There are times when one partner is simply unwilling or unable to make the changes necessary to improve the relationship. The most difficult question I am asked is when to give up hope and end the relationship. I simply do not have a good answer for this conundrum. I have found, however, that many people find it helpful to keep a journal of their feelings. When a person discovers that the concerns he is writing about are virtually identical to those he had recorded a year earlier, for example, he might decide that it is time to end the relationship, thinking that life is too short to give hope a free rein.

+ 3 +

how happy are you with your sex life?

The following phrases describe people's behaviors, attitudes, and feelings. Indicate the extent to which you agree that the statement describes you.

1. I am satisfied with the frequency with which I have sex.

1	2	3	4	5
strongly disagree	disagree	neither agree nor disagree	agree	strongly agree

2. My sexual encounters are very enjoyable for me.

1	2	3	4	5
strongly disagree	disagree	neither agree nor disagree	agree	strongly agree

3. There are some sexual experiences I have never had but wish I could have.

1	2	3	4	5
strongly disagree	disagree	neither agree nor disagree	agree	strongly agree

4. I wish I could have more sexual partners.

1	2	3	4	5
strongly disagree	disagree	neither agree nor disagree	agree	strongly agree

5. It is difficult for me to talk with my partner about sex.

1	2	3	4	5
strongly disagree	disagree	neither agree nor disagree	agree	strongly agree

6. My partner is extremely desirable.

1	2	3	4	5
strongly disagree	disagree	neither agree nor disagree	agree	strongly agree

7. I often feel sexually frustrated.

1	2	3	4	5
strongly disagree	disagree	neither agree nor disagree	agree	strongly agree

8. My partner and I enjoy exploring new ways of exciting each other.

1	2	3	4	5
strongly disagree	disagree	neither agree nor disagree	agree	strongly agree

9. I feel very close to my partner after we have sex.

1	2	3	4	5
strongly disagree	disagree	neither agree nor disagree	agree	strongly agree

10. After a sexual encounter, I would prefer to be alone.

1	2	3	4	5
strongly disagree	disagree	neither agree nor disagree	agree	strongly agree

11. I believe our society places too much emphasis on sex.

1	2	3	4	5
strongly disagree	disagree	neither agree nor disagree	agree	strongly agree

12. My partner and I have similar feelings about how often to have sex.

1	2	3	4	5
strongly disagree	disagree	neither agree nor disagree	agree	strongly agree

13. My partner is willing to try new things to please me sexually.

1	2	3	4	5
strongly disagree	disagree	neither agree nor disagree	agree	strongly agree

14. I am willing to try new things to please my partner sexually.

1	2	3	4	5
strongly disagree	disagree	neither agree nor disagree	agree	strongly agree

15. I would lie in order to have sex with someone I was interested in.

1	2	3	4	5
strongly disagree	disagree	neither agree nor disagree	agree	strongly agree

16. I feel guilty when I have sexual feelings.

1	2	3	4	5
strongly disagree	disagree	neither agree nor disagree	agree	strongly agree

17. I worry about sexually transmitted diseases.

1	2	3	4	5
strongly disagree	disagree	neither agree nor disagree	agree	strongly agree

18. When it comes to sex, I can talk to my partner about anything.

1	2	3	4	5
strongly disagree	disagree	neither agree nor disagree	agree	strongly agree

19. I know my partner finds me sexually attractive.

1	2	3	4	5
strongly disagree	disagree	neither agree nor disagree	agree	strongly agree

20. How I feel about my partner makes little difference in how much I enjoy having sex with him or her.

1	2	3	4	5
strongly disagree	disagree	neither agree nor disagree	agree	strongly agree

+ scoring

The first step is to reverse score items 3, 4, 7, 10, 11, 15, 16, 17, and 20. For these items, if you circled 5 change it to a 1, a 4 becomes a 2, a 3 remains a 3, a 2 becomes a 4, and a 1 becomes a 5. After you have made these changes, add your points together for your total score on the Sexual Experiences Test. High scores indicate a high level of satisfaction with your sex life.

SEXUAL EXPERIENCES SCORE	PERCENTILE
81	85
76	70
70	50
64	30
59	15

+ about the sexual experiences test

Sex is different from other human needs. While no one can survive, much less live happily, without water, food, and protection from the elements, we can live without sex. And although most of us would maintain that we cannot live happily without it, there are many who can and do. These people include not only religious figures but many ordinary men and women who experience their lives as complete and satisfying despite an absence of sexual experiences. And even among those people who believe that sex does play an important role in their happiness, there are an almost unlimited variety of ways in which people achieve their sexual satisfaction. For some people, once a month is plenty; for others, once a day is not enough. Some people find happiness in a long-term monogamous relationship, while others are continually looking for new partners. I'm sure that with a little imagination, you can think of many more examples of the variety of ways in which people seek sexual satisfaction.

Perhaps because of this diversity, psychologists have yet to document the link between sexuality and happiness, but we do know a few things. We know, for instance, that depressed people often lose interest in sex, so it seems reasonable to assume that happy people are more likely to be sexually active. But we still have much to learn about whether specific sexual lifestyles are more likely to lead to happiness than others. Like everyone else, I have my own ideas about this issue and the items on the Sexual Experiences Test reflect my views. It will take years before sufficient research has accumulated to determine if all my beliefs are justified, but let me share my thoughts with you.

First, several of the items on the scale were included to measure if you have a generally positive view of sex. Item 16 is an obvious example. If you indicated that you feel guilty about your sexual feelings, clearly, you do not have a positive view of sex. Items that may be more subtle, like 5, 13, 14, and 18, indicate feeling comfortable when talking about sex and a willingness to experiment and try new things. If you agreed with item 17, "I worry about sexually transmitted diseases," you also probably feel somewhat uncomfortable about sexual issues. People who have positive feelings about sex do not find it difficult to be sexually responsible. They can talk easily with prospective partners about their health status, will get tested if necessary, and are willing to use condoms when appropriate. Because people who feel completely comfortable with their sexuality find it easy to be sexually responsible, they do not have to worry about contacting a sexually transmitted disease. Having a positive view of sex and feeling comfortable with one's sexuality is a starting place. It is, I think, a necessary foundation for sexual happiness.

Most of the remaining questions on the scale reflect my belief that the surest road to sexual happiness over the long run is to have a sexual partner you care for deeply and whom you find attractive and exciting. I'm not sure there is a more gratifying human experience than to make love with someone you cherish and, afterwards, to hold each other close and simply be with each other. This ideal should not come as a surprise to anyone. I would bet that most everyone would agree that sex is best when it is expressed in the context of a loving relationship, so the important question is why so many of us fail to live up to a standard that we know is best for us.

I do not have any definitive answers, but my experiences in both teaching and clinical practice have suggested some possible answers. First, I do think that many people marry too early and, after a few years or even as long as a decade or two, conclude that they missed out on potentially exciting experiences. Erika, for instance, had one brief relationship during her sophomore year in college, then fell deeply in love with Brad, her husband-to-be, during her junior year. They were married shortly after they both graduated, and fifteen years of marriage later, Erika began to feel restless. "I love my husband," she would say without hesitation, "but I can't help wondering if my life might not be more exciting and fulfilling if I were single and free to have lots of different experiences." This feeling gnawed at her for two years before she succumbed and had an affair. Brad learned about her relationship and insisted on a divorce. Five years later Erika was remarried and happy in that relationship, but she wished things could have been different. "I love my second husband but life is so much more complicated now. Brad is also remarried and now we have to deal with all the problems associated with stepchildren. It's a real balancing act with grandparents, aunts, and uncles. My life has become so confusing and complicated."

Had Erika remained single for a few years and been able to experience both the pleasures and frustrations of getting to know a variety of people, perhaps she would have had the opportunity to mature and to understand how valuable what she had in her first marriage was. While most of us, at least on occasion, probably have fantasies of having casual but exciting sex with a string of beautiful partners, the reality is almost always disappointing. I'm not sure there is a more empty feeling than concluding a sexual encounter and not knowing what to say to your partner. And then wondering how long politeness demands that you stay before going home. I have yet to meet anyone who has reached at least his or her fifties who maintains that the way to happiness is to have a series of casual sexual relationships. On the other hand, I know many people in this age range who have maintained a stable and monogamous sexual relationship and who are very happy with their lives.

A second observation is that it is important to one's happiness to have a sexual partner who has similar ideas about sex to your own. As I mentioned earlier, there is an endless variety of ways in which people experience their sexuality, and couples who have very different sexual styles are likely to be unhappy. Perhaps the most common and contentious issue concerns frequency. Surveys have shown that among married couples, about 20 percent of both men and women wish they were having sex more often than they are. Many couples are able to reach a compromise, but others discover to their great frustration that being married does not necessarily guarantee an available and willing sex partner.

It is not always easy to predict whether a prospective spouse has sexual attitudes that are compatible with your own. People do change as the relationship progresses, sometimes in positive directions, sometimes in negative ways. Men and women saddled with guilt and anxiety can become enthusiastic sexual partners with the encouragement and support of a loving spouse. On the other hand, some people experience the flames of passion early in a relationship only to have them extinguished by the marriage ceremony. Even when couples' sexual needs change over the course of a long-term relationship, it is possible to accommodate these changes so long as both spouses are willing to discuss their needs in an open and loving way.

I have known people, however, who ignored clear warning signs only to regret it later. Lee was engaged to a man for nearly two years, and while she was concerned by his lack of interest in most any form of physical affection, she convinced herself that he would change once they were married and committed to each other. As you might have guessed, he did not. After a couple of years, Lee found herself crying frequently, wondering why her husband did not find her attractive, why he did not love her the way she loved him. I believe the most important thing that Lee could have done—that anyone can do—is find a partner who has similar attitudes and values about sex. A comfortable, loving sexual relationship may not guarantee happiness, but it can go a long way to helping us find it.

+ 4 +

are you part of a big, happy family?

The following phrases describe people's behaviors, attitudes, and feelings. Indicate the extent to which you agree that the statement describes you.

1. My father is [was] a good man.

1	2	3	4	5
strongly disagree	disagree	neither agree nor disagree	agree	strongly agree

2. I get together with my family during the holidays.

1	2	3	4	5
strongly disagree	disagree	neither agree nor disagree	agree	strongly agree

3. I enjoy family get-togethers.

1	2	3	4	5
strongly disagree	disagree	neither agree nor disagree	agree	strongly agree

4. I have relatives whom I try to avoid.

1	2	3	4	5
strongly disagree	disagree	neither agree nor disagree	agree	strongly agree

5. Family bonds are stronger than friendship.

1	2	3	4	5
strongly disagree	disagree	neither agree nor disagree	agree	strongly agree

6. When I have a problem I talk it over with a family member.

1	2	3	4	5
strongly disagree	disagree	neither agree nor disagree	agree	strongly agree

7. My mother is [was] a good person.

1	2	3	4	5
strongly disagree	disagree	neither agree nor disagree	agree	strongly agree

8. My family is the center of my life.

1	2	3	4	5
strongly disagree	disagree	neither agree nor disagree	agree	strongly agree

9. I enjoy hearing my grandparents tell stories about the old days.

1	2	3	4	5
strongly disagree	disagree	neither agree nor disagree	agree	strongly agree

10. I am proud of my family.

1	2	3	4	5
strongly disagree	disagree	neither agree nor disagree	agree	strongly agree

11. I visit a family member at least once per week.

1	2	3	4	5
strongly disagree	disagree	neither agree nor disagree	agree	strongly agree

12. I could not have accomplished as much as I have without the help and support of my family.

1	2	3	4	5
strongly disagree	disagree	neither agree nor disagree	agree	strongly agree

13. My family get-togethers are often awkward and uncomfortable.

1	2	3	4	5
strongly disagree	disagree	neither agree nor disagree	agree	strongly agree

14. I would be happier if I did not have to see certain members of my family.

1	2	3	4	5
strongly disagree	disagree	neither agree nor disagree	agree	strongly agree

15. During difficult times, I can count on my family for help.

1	2	3	4	5
strongly disagree	disagree	neither agree nor disagree	agree	strongly agree

16. I have regular contact with family members who live far away.

1	2	3	4	5
strongly disagree	disagree	neither agree nor disagree	agree	strongly agree

17. I spend much of my vacation time with family members.

1	2	3	4	5
strongly disagree	disagree	neither agree nor disagree	agree	strongly agree

18. I have cut off contact with at least one member of my family.

1	2	3	4	5
strongly disagree	disagree	neither agree nor disagree	agree	strongly agree

19. I will [do] take care of my parents if they cannot care for themselves.

1	2	3	4	5
strongly disagree	disagree	neither agree nor disagree	agree	strongly agree

20. I am happily married.

1	2	3	4	5
strongly disagree	disagree	neither agree nor disagree	agree	strongly agree

+ scoring

The first step is to reverse score items 4, 13, 14, and 18. For these items, if you circled 5, change it to a 1, a 4 becomes a 2, a 3 remains a 3, a 2 becomes a 4, and a 1 becomes a 5. After you have made these changes, add your points together for your total score on the Family Satisfaction Test. High scores indicate a high degree of family satisfaction.

FAMILY SATISFACTION SCORE	PERCENTILE
78	85
71	70
64	50
57	30
50	15

+ about the family relationships test

Families play a fundamental role in our lives. They can be our primary source of strength and affection, or they can cause us immeasurable pain and misery. And to some extent, whether we have the first experience or the second is a matter of chance. After all, as the old saying goes, we can choose our friends but we can't choose our family. Although it may seem to those of you who received low scores on the family relationships test that we're stuck with what we get, we do have the ability to move past the hurt and misery of bad family relationships and begin our own tradition of a kind, supportive, and loving family. Even if you are a person whose mother or father caused you immeasurable pain or who has cut off all contact with a family member, you are not doomed to have unhappy family relationships forever. You can start fresh and begin a new tradition for your children. It will help make you all happier people.

The first step in developing healthy family relationships is to have a happy, solid marriage. Despite the fact that a substantial percentage of marriages in our society end in divorce, which would seem to suggest that married people are a miserable lot, the truth is that married people are happier and healthier than the unmarried. And despite the endless jokes about nagging wives and feckless husbands, most of us believe that we would be happier married to a decent person than alone and single. More than 90 percent of us will marry at least once, and a substantial majority of us who divorce will marry again. We seem to crave the security and comfort that can come from this most important of all family relationships.

To increase the odds of long-term happiness, it is important to pay attention to your prospective spouse's family relationships before making a commitment. If he or she has nothing but bad things to say about parents and siblings, the odds are this person will not make it easy for you to have happy family relationships in the future. There are, of course, many people who are justified in having bad things to say about their family, but even if these feelings are based on reality, or perhaps because of that reality, it is likely that such a person will have stormy family relationships in the future. You would be wise to look for a spouse who treats his or her parents with love and respect, a spouse who values the parents' advice but does not feel compelled to follow all their dictates. (Indeed, you would be well advised to avoid a spouse who has parents who issue dictates.) Attend your prospective spouse's family gatherings. If people there seem to like each other and enjoy each other's company, it would be a good sign that your spouse would increase your odds of having happy family relationships.

The next step to having good family relationships concerns children. It is interesting that people who have children are no more or no less happy than those without children. But this net result of "no effect" results from the many people whose children increase their happiness being balanced out by those whose children bring them pain and sadness. While there are certainly cases in which children have brought pain to devoted and loving parents, this is generally an area in which we reap what we sow. Vincent, for example, spent the last decade of his life bitter because his four children almost never visited him and rarely remembered to send so much as a card on his birthday. When his children were young, he worked long hours and then spent many of his evenings unwinding with his friends. He attended school plays, scouting ceremonies, and the like about as often as his children visited him in his later years. When he did talk to his children, it was mostly to criticize them or tell them to be quiet so he could hear the ball game on the TV. It is little wonder that his children do not visit him. They see him as a stranger, and an ill-tempered one at that.

Research psychologists have found that the relationship between parents and children is rarely smooth sailing for even the best of parents. There is a predictable relationship between the happiness of the parents and the age of their children. The unhappiest parents are those with very young children. As excited as most parents are at the prospective birth of their children, they soon learn that having babies is very hard work and that it may be years before they can go through a day without feeling irritable and sleep deprived. This is not to say that having babies is not without its joys. Many of my most pleasurable memories go back to when my two boys were very young. I still remember vividly the way Christopher's eyes became big and round the first time he tasted a peach. But I was constantly tired for about three years, and while there were many moments of pure happiness, there were even more times when I wondered if I would ever be able to read a novel again.

Parents' happiness levels gradually increase as their children grow older, and then there is another dip when they become teenagers. Again, there are at least a handful of parents who have had perfect teenagers (I was not one of the fortunate few); but most of us have at least some experience with the dark side of this developmental period—the natural but distressing time when children feel a need to assert their independence, the time when they know their parents are barely competent and that their friends are the ultimate source of wisdom. Most parents make it through this time relatively unscathed and experience a dramatic increase in their happiness when their children leave home if the children stay in contact. Parents who rarely see their children after they leave home experience a decline in their happiness, so it is crucial to build a solid family foundation so your children will want to have a relationship with you.

There is little research to guide us when it comes to extended families other than the finding that people in societies that place a high value on family do appear to benefit from this. I believe it is worthwhile to try to maintain a good relationship with your extended family, though in today's society I understand all too well how difficult this can be. It was much easier for our parents and grandparents when everyone in the family spent most of their lives in the community in which they were born. But today's families are different. I am among this new breed, with a brother who lives three thousand miles away and a sister and parents who live two thousand miles away. My cousins have scattered across the country, and it has been several years since I last saw any of them.

It seems to me that those families who have regular gatherings despite the distances have at least one member who is willing to take the responsibility and make the effort to see that it does happen regularly. I envy the families who view their large gatherings as the high point of their year, but those of us who do not have this experience can place a high value on the family relationships that we do have. My personal experience confirms the research finding that families are an important source of life satisfaction and happiness.

+ 5 +

how well do you get along with others?

The following phrases describe people's behaviors, attitudes, and feelings. Indicate the extent to which you agree that the statement describes you.

1. Sometimes I enjoy obstructing others' plans.

1	2	3	4	5
strongly disagree	disagree	neither agree nor disagree	agree	strongly agree

2. I am easy to please.

1	2	3	4	5
strongly disagree	disagree	neither agree nor disagree	agree	strongly agree

3. I like to be the center of attention.

1	2	3	4	5
strongly disagree	disagree	neither agree nor disagree	agree	strongly agree

4. I try to avoid confrontations.

1	2	3	4	5
strongly disagree	disagree	neither agree nor disagree	agree	strongly agree

5. I pride myself on following the rules.

1	2	3	4	5
strongly disagree	disagree	neither agree nor disagree	agree	strongly agree

6. I do not like to talk about myself.

1	2	3	4	5
strongly disagree	disagree	neither agree nor disagree	agree	strongly agree

7. Sometimes it is necessary to take advantage of others.

1	2	3	4	5
strongly disagree	disagree	neither agree nor disagree	agree	strongly agree

8. I have been known to have a sharp tongue.

1	2	3	4	5
strongly disagree	disagree	neither agree nor disagree	agree	strongly agree

9. I enjoy telling others about my accomplishments.

1	2	3	4	5
strongly disagree	disagree	neither agree nor disagree	agree	strongly agree

10. I feel more comfortable in situations that demand cooperation over competition.

1	2	3	4	5
strongly disagree	disagree	neither agree nor disagree	agree	strongly agree

11. I enjoy a good argument.

1	2	3	4	5
strongly disagree	disagree	neither agree nor disagree	agree	strongly agree

12. Sometimes I yell at other people.

1	2	3	4	5
strongly disagree	disagree	neither agree nor disagree	agree	strongly agree

13. If necessary, I will bend the rules to get ahead.

1	2	3	4	5
strongly disagree	disagree	neither agree nor disagree	agree	strongly agree

14. I try to make people feel comfortable.

1	2	3	4	5
strongly disagree	disagree	neither agree nor disagree	agree	strongly agree

15. I believe that people are basically good.

1	2	3	4	5
strongly disagree	disagree	neither agree nor disagree	agree	strongly agree

16. I tend to feel superior to others.

1	2	3	4	5
strongly disagree	disagree	neither agree nor disagree	agree	strongly agree

17. People should not depend on others.

1	2	3	4	5
strongly disagree	disagree	neither agree nor disagree	agree	strongly agree

18. Soft-hearted people are weak.

1	2	3	4	5
strongly disagree	disagree	neither agree nor disagree	agree	strongly agree

19. It is easy for me to find something good to say about most everyone.

1	2	3	4	5
strongly disagree	disagree	neither agree nor disagree	agree	strongly agree

20. If someone wrongs me I try to get back at him or her.

1	2	3	4	5
strongly disagree	disagree	neither agree nor disagree	agree	strongly agree

+ scoring

The first step is to reverse score items 1, 3, 7, 8, 9, 11, 12, 13, 16, 17, 18, and 20. For these items, if you circled 5, change it to a 1, a 4 becomes a 2, a 3 remains a 3, a 2 becomes a 4, and a 1 becomes a 5. After you have made these changes, add your points together for your total score on the Agreeableness Test. High scores indicate a high level of agreeableness.

AGREEABLENESS SCORE	PERCENTILE
84	**85**
75	70
66	**50**
57	30
48	**15**

+ about the agreeableness test

Agreeable people are motivated to have close, rewarding relationships with others. They place a high value on getting along with their family, friends, and acquaintances, and they generally believe that having solid relationships is more important than achieving success. Agreeable people are seen by others as being nice guys, the kind of people that you would be happy to have as friends. And because close, satisfying relationships are so important to a sense of well-being, agreeable people are likely to be happier than their less agreeable counterparts. If you received a score below the 30th percentile, you may be able to increase your happiness by becoming a more agreeable person.

The key to being an agreeable person is, I think, having the perspective that all of us are in this thing we call life together. Sure, some of us are smarter than others, some of us have more education or more money than others, but in the final analysis we have to depend on each other if we are to make the short time we have on this earth count for something. Agreeable people do not have a sense of superiority; they do not think of themselves as better than others. They certainly do not view others as sources to be exploited or as vehicles to be used to get ahead. They see others as their equals, as deserving of their respect and consideration.

One interesting characteristic of agreeable people is that they have only moderately high self-esteem. Pop psychology has placed so much emphasis on self-esteem that no one could be blamed for believing that the higher one's self esteem, the better, but research has shown that this is true only to a point. It is certainly true that low self-esteem is related to a variety of maladies. People who have very negative views of themselves are more likely to be depressed, to be anxious, to have poor relationships with others, and to perform poorly in both academic and vocational settings. But there are also dangers associated with having excessively high self-esteem. Such people can be egotistical to the point of arrogance and can be contemptuous of others.

Barry was one of these people. A very successful divorce attorney, Barry took pride in his reputation as the meanest s.o.b. in town. And, indeed, being the meanest s.o.b. in town undoubtedly contributed to his success. Barry never considered issues such as fairness or morality; he was interested only in obtaining the best possible settlement for his client, which, in turn, enhanced his reputation. He could be extremely intimidating during negotiation sessions, and he never hesitated to embarrass or humiliate his opponent during hearings if it advanced his case to do so. Barry's sense of superiority carried over in his personal relationships. He believed he was smarter and more capable than anyone he knew, and he had little patience for the opinions of others. What might begin as a casual social conversation usually ended with yet another pedantic lecture from Barry. Most everyone who knew him thought that Barry would be better off if his self-esteem were reduced by half.

It is interesting that Barry saw himself as an agreeable person. He claimed that his mean, arrogant persona was something that he had to use on his job but that he got along with others quite well in social situations. He was wrong. He confused extroversion with agreeableness. While it was true that he could talk to others easily, others did not enjoy talking to him; in fact, they actively avoided him. And had Barry been honest with himself, he would have acknowledged that there were times when he felt lonely but had no one to call. He would dismiss these moments by telling himself that he was too busy and too successful to have a social life.

I don't believe it is possible to have two sides to your personality, as Barry claimed he had. Truly agreeable people carry their worldview with them regardless of whether they are at work or with family and friends. They treat their business colleagues with the same respect and consideration they give to others. Agreeableness must be authentic to be meaningful. It cannot be a role we adopt for certain situations.

Some of you may have scored above the 50th percentile but find that others are not able to recognize that in your heart you are an agreeable person. While it is not necessary to be an extrovert to be happy, it is important to be sufficiently outgoing so that others can see your desirable qualities. Corine was like this. She genuinely liked other people and never said a mean word to anyone, but she was so quiet and reserved that only a handful of people understood the kind of person she was. Most of her colleagues simply saw her as very reserved and someone who preferred to be left to herself. If you see similarities between yourself and Corine, pay special attention to the discussion in Chapter 1. You need to take chances, to speak up, to let others know what is inside of you. You have what it takes to be liked and to have close satisfying relationships, but you have to give others the opportunity to discover those qualities. With effort and persistence, you can learn to reveal more of yourself; and as you do, you will reap the benefits that connecting with others can yield.

There is a downside to agreeableness, at least according to the perspective of some. Our friend Barry was not an exception; people who are low in agreeableness do achieve greater success in some occupations than their high-scoring colleagues. Effective managers, for instance, tend to be at least moderately low in agreeableness. They often have to make difficult decisions that will result in others' suffering. An agreeable manager might find it nearly impossible to fire the single mother of five who desperately needs a job, whereas the manager low in agreeableness would not hesitate to do so if she were not an effective employee. And because agreeable people place a premium on cooperation, they may not have the requisite drive and single-mindedness to excel in their field. This is a trade-off that not everyone is willing to make.

In my mind, there is not much of a question as to which style is more likely to result in happiness. As we grow older and approach our twilight years, I think we all want to be surrounded by loving family and friends. Relationships really are the key to a satisfying and fulfilling life. I have not seen any research that has found that outstanding success is associated with happiness, but there are countless studies that demonstrate the importance of family and friends. While I would agree that we have to be competent at what we do in order to feel good about ourselves, a relentless climb up the ladder of success alone is unlikely to get us to where we want to be.

I do not mean to trivialize this trade-off; it can mean difficult choices. I have asked a number of people the following question, and you might find it interesting to give it some thought. Suppose you had the option of feeling happy and joyful every day of your life even though you worked at a minimum-wage job or you could achieve worldwide fame at whatever you would love to do but your days would be sad and lonely. I have yet to have anyone choose happiness without hesitation. The point is that if we are to have any chance of being happy, we have to make it our top priority. Without clear priorities, we are likely to be trapped by the countless occasions when we have to choose between some momentary gratification and our long-term happiness.

PART TWO

material world

+ + +

+ 6 +

are you happy at work?

The following phrases describe people's behaviors, attitudes, and feelings. Indicate the extent to which you agree that the statement describes you.

1. If I knew I could find another one, I would quit my job today.

1	2	3	4	5
strongly disagree	disagree	neither agree nor disagree	agree	strongly agree

2. I believe my job makes an important contribution to society.

1	2	3	4	5
strongly disagree	disagree	neither agree nor disagree	agree	strongly agree

3. I like my job more than most people like theirs.

1	2	3	4	5
strongly disagree	disagree	neither agree nor disagree	agree	strongly agree

4. I am in a good mood when I begin the workweek.

1	2	3	4	5
strongly disagree	disagree	neither agree nor disagree	agree	strongly agree

5. I wish I had selected a different occupation.

1	2	3	4	5
strongly disagree	disagree	neither agree nor disagree	agree	strongly agree

6. When I am at work I feel that my education is being wasted.

1	2	3	4	5
strongly disagree	disagree	neither agree nor disagree	agree	strongly agree

7. My work is a very important part of who I am.

1	2	3	4	5
strongly disagree	disagree	neither agree nor disagree	agree	strongly agree

8. I enjoy the challenges my job presents.

1	2	3	4	5
strongly disagree	disagree	neither agree nor disagree	agree	strongly agree

9. If I were rich, I would never work another day.

1	2	3	4	5
strongly disagree	disagree	neither agree nor disagree	agree	strongly agree

10. Most of my personal goals are related to my work.

1	2	3	4	5
strongly disagree	disagree	neither agree nor disagree	agree	strongly agree

11. I am good at my job.

1	2	3	4	5
strongly disagree	disagree	neither agree nor disagree	agree	strongly agree

12. When I am at work, the time passes very quickly.

1	2	3	4	5
strongly disagree	disagree	neither agree nor disagree	agree	strongly agree

13. I get along well with my supervisor.

1	2	3	4	5
strongly disagree	disagree	neither agree nor disagree	agree	strongly agree

14. I do not get the recognition I deserve at work.

1	2	3	4	5
strongly disagree	disagree	neither agree nor disagree	agree	strongly agree

15. I feel I have to be careful about what I say at meetings.

1	2	3	4	5
strongly disagree	disagree	neither agree nor disagree	agree	strongly agree

16. My opinion matters in how things are done in my company.

1	2	3	4	5
strongly disagree	disagree	neither agree nor disagree	agree	strongly agree

17. I do not have enough time to get everything done that I am expected to do at work.

1	2	3	4	5
strongly disagree	disagree	neither agree nor disagree	agree	strongly agree

18. My co-workers do not do their share.

1	2	3	4	5
strongly disagree	disagree	neither agree nor disagree	agree	strongly agree

19. My supervisor does not make clear what he expects of me.

1	2	3	4	5
strongly disagree	disagree	neither agree nor disagree	agree	strongly agree

20. I feel a great deal of stress at work.

1	2	3	4	5
strongly disagree	disagree	neither agree nor disagree	agree	strongly agree

+ scoring

The first step is to reverse score items 1, 5, 6, 9, 14, 15, 17, 18, 19, and 20. For these items, if you circled 5, change it to a 1, a 4 becomes a 2, a 3 remains a 3, a 2 becomes a 4, and a 1 becomes a 5.

This test consists of two scales, a Career Satisfaction scale and a Stress Management scale. To find your career satisfaction score, add your points for items 1 through 12. To find your Stress Management score, add your points for items 13 through 20. High scores indicate a high level of job satisfaction and little stress at work.

SATISFACTION	STRESS MANAGEMENT	PERCENTILE
49	34	85
45	30	70
40	26	50
35	22	30
31	18	15

+ about the career test

It has been said that there are three ways in which people can view their work. First are those who have jobs. They work because they have to, because they need the money. Some of these people hate their jobs, others find them tolerable, but all of them would quit on a moment's notice if they suddenly became financially independent. The second group of people have careers. They work for the financial rewards and the status. They measure their success with raises and promotions. While these people can find their work highly satisfying for many years, many of them will eventually become disillusioned and even alienated. Because only a few make it to the very top, when the raises and promotions come to an end, as they inevitably do for the majority, these people are forced to find satisfaction and meaning in other areas of their lives. The third category consists of people for whom work is a calling. These fortunate people are passionate about their work. They find it meaningful and involving. They work for the sake of the work, and the money and status are largely irrelevant. These are the people who would show up for work the day after winning the lottery. Obviously, those who find their work to be a calling are likely to be the happiest.

While most of us hope our children will become doctors, lawyers, or the like, with the belief that happiness will come with success, you might be surprised to learn that the status of an occupation and the satisfaction of those in it are only modestly related. Although it is true that blue-collar workers tend to be somewhat more satisfied with their jobs than unskilled workers, and professionals tend to be more satisfied than white-collar workers, there are both satisfied and dissatisfied workers at every level. I've known physicians who hated their jobs, and I've known blue-collar workers who found their work to be a calling. My dad was one of these people. He was a carpenter who loved his work and took great pride in it. Once his children were adults and owned their own homes, he would bring his tools along when he visited so they could live in more functional and beautiful settings.

Martin Seligman, perhaps the most prominent theorist in the field of positive psychology, wrote that finding meaning in one's work is crucial to happiness, and he eloquently pointed out that this meaning can be found at any rung on the status ladder. I have seen this myself. I have known college professors who clearly view their work as a job. They complain about uninterested and unmotivated students and view most of their responsibilities as onerous burdens. On the other hand, I have met orderlies who worked in a nursing home who believed their jobs were very important. Yes, many of them were there because they could not find higher-paying work, but others believed that every day offered the opportunity to make life better for the residents. As one young man described it: "Many of the people here never have anyone come to visit them. Can you imagine what it must feel like to be near the end of your life and feel all alone in the world? If I can let them know that I care about how they are doing or if I can make them laugh, I've made their day a little better and I've helped them feel a little less alone."

If you received a low score on the Career Satisfaction Test, you have two options. The first is to change your job—either your vocation or the setting in which you work. If you are dissatisfied with your vocation, decide what you would like to do and make a plan to get there. This may require years of sacrifice and hard work, but the payoff can be enormous. And it is never too late to start. One woman I know began to take night classes at the university when she was in her early forties. Soon she quit her clerical job and, a few months before her fiftieth birthday, enrolled as a full-time student in our doctoral program. Today, she is a practicing clinical psychologist who views her work as a calling.

The second option for those who scored low on this scale is to change the way you view your work. Hospital orderlies can value their contacts with patients and see the importance of their contributions to making the health care system work. Teachers can treasure the opportunity to influence the lives of their students while understanding that there will always be children they cannot reach. I believe that it is possible to find meaning in almost every job, although I confess I do not know what suggestions I would make to telephone solicitors.

If you received a low score on the Stress Management Test,

you also have the two options of changing your job or changing the way you view your job. Sometimes it can be difficult to know which is the better strategy. For instance, I would score very low on days when I see the university administrators changing the rules without consulting the faculty or rewarding professors who generate large grants more than those who are effective teachers. On those bad days, when I experience stress, I remind myself to make my own personal attitude adjustment. I know that other universities are pretty much the same as mine and, despite my occasional frustrations, I have a great deal of freedom to pursue my own interests (such as writing this book) even if they are not directly benefiting the university. I remind myself of the deep sense of satisfaction I experience when I talk with bright, motivated students and the excitement I feel when planning a new project with a colleague. I know that moving to another university would not reduce my stress, so the better option is to change the way I view my job.

There are times when the better option is to change jobs. Some organizations are toxic, some supervisors are abusive, and some colleagues are impossible. Stan was a mechanic at a car dealership, and his stomach would tighten into knots on the way to work each morning. Although he was never explicitly asked to make unnecessary repairs, he was pressured to "find" problems, especially when the car had a few miles on it. He did not like having to convince customers to pay for maintenance services that he believed were of little value, and he had shouting matches with his supervisor over his refusal to certify the soundness of used cars when he had not inspected them. Stan experienced so much stress that he came to the conclusion that becoming a mechanic had been a mistake. After taking several months off to hike the Appalachian Trial and to think about his options, he risked his entire savings to rent a modest shop at the edge of the city. His stress level reached new highs when he failed to attract a single customer the first four days of business, but his integrity and his firm belief in the importance of his work was obvious to all who knew him. Before long, word of mouth began to have its effect, and six months after opening his shop Stan was hoping to hire a second mechanic so he would not have to turn away so much business. He had never felt happier.

Most of us will spend more time working than in any other activity, with the likely exception of sleeping. So, obviously, finding satisfaction in our work is critical to our life satisfaction and happiness. To those of you who had low scores on both parts of the career test, I hope I don't sound glib when I say that you only have two options—to change your work or to change your attitude about your work. The options are simple. Though I fully appreciate how difficult it can be to implement them, it can be done. Decide which option is appropriate for you and then develop a plan for achieving your goal. Use the other chapters in this book to identify your strengths and use them in your endeavor to change. If you are persistent, you will surely succeed.

+ 7 +

does your lifestyle make you happy?

The following phrases describe people's behaviors, attitudes, and feelings. Indicate the extent to which you agree that the statement describes you.

1. The kind of people I admire most are those who make a contribution to society.

1	2	3	4	5
strongly disagree	disagree	neither agree nor disagree	agree	strongly agree

2. I have close friends who have much less than I do.

1	2	3	4	5
strongly disagree	disagree	neither agree nor disagree	agree	strongly agree

3. It is difficult to be close friends with people who have very different financial circumstances than your own.

1	2	3	4	5
strongly disagree	disagree	neither agree nor disagree	agree	strongly agree

4. I would be embarrassed to be seen at a family-style restaurant.

1	2	3	4	5
strongly disagree	disagree	neither agree nor disagree	agree	strongly agree

5. It makes me happy to buy extravagant things.

1	2	3	4	5
strongly disagree	disagree	neither agree nor disagree	agree	strongly agree

6. It is important to me to have the right kind of friends.

1	2	3	4	5
strongly disagree	disagree	neither agree nor disagree	agree	strongly agree

7. I would be willing to make sacrifices to be able to drive a high-status car.

1	2	3	4	5
strongly disagree	disagree	neither agree nor disagree	agree	strongly agree

8. I would never consider wearing anything that was purchased from a discount store.

1	2	3	4	5
strongly disagree	disagree	neither agree nor disagree	agree	strongly agree

9. I am willing to sacrifice my time to help a friend.

1	2	3	4	5
strongly disagree	disagree	neither agree nor disagree	agree	strongly agree

10. I participate in volunteer work.

1	2	3	4	5
strongly disagree	disagree	neither agree nor disagree	agree	strongly agree

11. I envy people who have acquired a great deal of wealth.

1	2	3	4	5
strongly disagree	disagree	neither agree nor disagree	agree	strongly agree

12. I would much rather belong to a private club (such as a golf, tennis, or exercise club) than to use public facilities.

1	2	3	4	5
strongly disagree	disagree	neither agree nor disagree	agree	strongly agree

13. It is important to project an image of success.

1	2	3	4	5
strongly disagree	disagree	neither agree nor disagree	agree	strongly agree

14. If I had to spend my retirement years in a small apartment, I would feel like a failure.

1	2	3	4	5
strongly disagree	disagree	neither agree nor disagree	agree	strongly agree

15. I usually buy only things that I need.

1	2	3	4	5
strongly disagree	disagree	neither agree nor disagree	agree	strongly agree

16. I try to befriend the right kind of people.

1	2	3	4	5
strongly disagree	disagree	neither agree nor disagree	agree	strongly agree

17. I know I should spend more time with my family.

1	2	3	4	5
strongly disagree	disagree	neither agree nor disagree	agree	strongly agree

18. I enjoy sharing what I have with others.

1	2	3	4	5
strongly disagree	disagree	neither agree nor disagree	agree	strongly agree

19. I would be very upset if a child visiting my home broke one of my possessions.

1	2	3	4	5
strongly disagree	disagree	neither agree nor disagree	agree	strongly agree

20. I would never give money to a beggar.

1	2	3	4	5
strongly disagree	disagree	neither agree nor disagree	agree	strongly agree

21. It doesn't particularly bother me to lose something.

1	2	3	4	5
strongly disagree	disagree	neither agree nor disagree	agree	strongly agree

22. My idea of a perfect evening is talking with a group of close friends.

1	2	3	4	5
strongly disagree	disagree	neither agree nor disagree	agree	strongly agree

+ scoring

The first step is to reverse score items 3, 4, 5, 6, 7, 8, 11, 12, 13, 14, 16, 17, 19, and 20. For these items, if you circled 5, change it to a 1, a 4 becomes a 2, a 3 remains a 3, a 2 becomes a 4, and a 1 becomes a 5. After you have made these changes, add your points together for your total score on the Lifestyle Test. High scores indicate a lifestyle that promotes happiness.

LIFESTYLE SCORE	PERCENTILE
81	85
75	70
68	50
61	30
55	15

+ about the lifestyle test

Our society encourages us to have a materialistic lifestyle. Indeed, our economy depends on it. Beginning at a very early age, we are exposed to commercials that promote a longing for that special toy, that special possession. And as we grow older, we are bombarded with even more messages that attempt to convince us that our convenience, our hygiene, our sexiness, our very worth as a human being depend on buying the right products. No wonder most of us long to achieve success, to wear the right clothes, to drive the right car, to own the right house in the right neighborhood, even to have the right pet. And we transmit this message to our children too. While we pay lip service to the idea that all we want is for them to be happy, we pressure them to study hard so they can attend the best schools and be successful. *Success,* of course, means that one has the ability to buy the right clothes, the right car, etc. I am struck by the number of people I know who, when talking about their children, provide endless details about their career success and material acquisitions but say almost nothing about whether they are happy in their marriages or if they take joy in their children and friends.

Success and happiness are not mutually exclusive, but there is abundant evidence that having a materialistic lifestyle makes happiness elusive. Psychologist Tim Kasser, who has reviewed this research as well as conducted a number of his own investigations, has argued that people who do not hold materialistic values are happier, more satisfied with their lives, and less likely to suffer from a psychological disorder than those with a materialistic lifestyle. Furthermore, this is true not only for our society but also for people living in twelve other countries where this type of research has been done, such as Germany, India,

China, Russia, and Australia. Our society is far from alone in promoting a materialistic lifestyle.

According to Kasser, there are three components of materialism. The first of these is possessiveness, as represented in items 5, 7, and 21. It is important to materialistic people to own things, especially the "right" things, and their possessions are more important to them than the people in their lives. We have all known people who, if you asked to borrow their car, would react as if you were asking them to give you their youngest child. Such people are much more concerned about losing their possessions than about losing friends. Kasser's second component of materialism is nongenerosity, as reflected in items 9, 18, and 20. I'm not sure why this should be, and there do seem to be plenty of exceptions. Bill Gates must have a materialistic streak, or he would not be living in a house that is worth more than the gross national product of several countries, but he has also contributed huge amounts of money to worthy causes. I suspect that Gates's wealth is simply a by-product of the passion he has for his work. But Kasser's research has shown that materialistic people do not like donating things to charity or doing favors for friends. They always seem to be looking out for number one. Envy, as reflected in item 11, is the third component of materialism. Materialistic people are especially likely to feel bad when their friends, or even strangers, have more than they do. Their self-worth depends on their possessions; and if others have more, materialistic people are left with the feeling that they have failed.

One effect of a materialistic view of the world is that it leads to the perception of other people as objects, as resources that have the potential to be used to further one's own ends. These people may have an active social life, but it has to include the right kind of people. They must play golf or tennis at the club rather than the public courses or courts so they can associate with the right kind of people. They could not imagine spending an evening with someone whose position on the status ladder was much lower than their own, no matter how interesting such a person might be. And if they are to attract the right kind of people, they have to have to project the right image by wearing the right kind of clothes and driving the right kind of car.

Psychologist Ken Sheldon and his colleagues conducted an ingenious experiment demonstrating that materialistic people tend to view others as potential resources to be exploited. They asked college students to bring three friends to the laboratory to play a game called The Prisoner's Dilemma. If you watch *Law & Order,* you have a good idea what this is. Two prisoners are questioned separately, and if they stick to their stories and support each other, they both receive moderate prison terms. But if one agrees to testify against the other, he receives a very light sentence but his partner receives a lengthy one. In Sheldon's experiment, all four participants could win modest prizes through complete cooperation, but if one person turned against the other three, he or she could win much larger prizes. However, if two or more of the friends chose not to cooperate, all their prizes would be much smaller. As you might expect, the materialistic students were much more likely to sacrifice cooperation in their attempt to win larger prizes. They were willing to exploit their friends to win more movie tickets. And because the friends of materialistic students tended to be materialistic themselves, they all ended up winning small prizes because they were all using the same strategy: selling out their friends with the hope of winning more movie tickets. It is ironic and instructive that the nonmaterialistic students ended up winning more movie tickets because their friends had similar values and, generally, they all cooperated.

It would take several pages to list all the experts who agree that the most important factor associated with happiness is a feeling of connectedness with other people. So, if you received a low score on this scale, the most effective strategy would be to try to reduce your need for things and your need to be with the right kind of people and to try to increase the richness of your relationships with others. Begin with your family; they should be at the top of your priority list. I know a retired professor who was extraordinarily successful, but in the process of spending evenings and weekends working on his research, he alienated his wife and children. Now, he told me with a bitter chuckle, he spends most of his holidays reading his reprints. We have all heard the cliché that no one on his deathbed wishes to have spent more time at the office. So rather than spending a couple of extra hours trying to win the contract, spend it with your spouse and your children. Spend the time talking with them, communicating your love for them.

Low scorers should make friends and even acquaintances a bigger part of their lifestyle. The happiest people I know are those that have frequent, informal gatherings of friends. And they choose their friends because they are interesting and caring, not because they are the "right" kind of people. Happy people seem to have a need to connect with most of the people they come into contact with. I have noticed that my happy colleagues know the cleaning people by name. I see them chatting in the hall, talking about their respective weekends. The dour professors barely nod to these people, even after seeing them every day for years.

If you received a low score on this test, it will be difficult for you to change. But keep in mind that by reading this book you are acknowledging that you may have behaviors that undermine your own happiness. And as so many have said before, the first step to making meaningful changes is to recognize the need to do so. So taking these tests is an important first step. You can overcome the materialism that is making you unhappy by cutting back on your purchases, sharing your good fortune as well as your time with others, and, above all else, connecting with the people in your life. I promise you won't be sorry.

are you happy with your financial situation?

The following phrases describe people's behaviors, attitudes, and feelings. Indicate the extent to which you agree that the statement describes you.

1. Sometimes I am hungry because I do not have enough money to buy food.

1	2	3	4	5
strongly disagree	disagree	neither agree nor disagree	agree	strongly agree

2. I do not care what kind of car I drive as long as it is reliable.

1	2	3	4	5
strongly disagree	disagree	neither agree nor disagree	agree	strongly agree

3. I wish I could afford to live in a nicer house.

1	2	3	4	5
strongly disagree	disagree	neither agree nor disagree	agree	strongly agree

4. I cannot afford to have my own place to live.

1	2	3	4	5
strongly disagree	disagree	neither agree nor disagree	agree	strongly agree

5. I never have enough money to pay all the bills at the end of the month.

1	2	3	4	5
strongly disagree	disagree	neither agree nor disagree	agree	strongly agree

6. I am financially independent.

1	2	3	4	5
strongly disagree	disagree	neither agree nor disagree	agree	strongly agree

7. Sometimes I am cold because I cannot afford to pay the utility bill.

1	2	3	4	5
strongly disagree	disagree	neither agree nor disagree	agree	strongly agree

8. I feel bad because I do not earn as much money as most of my friends.

1	2	3	4	5
strongly disagree	disagree	neither agree nor disagree	agree	strongly agree

9. My partner sometimes gets angry at me because I spend more money than I should.

1	2	3	4	5
strongly disagree	disagree	neither agree nor disagree	agree	strongly agree

10. I cannot afford to buy clothes to keep me warm in the winter.

1	2	3	4	5
strongly disagree	disagree	neither agree nor disagree	agree	strongly agree

11. I often fantasize about what it would be like to be rich.

1	2	3	4	5
strongly disagree	disagree	neither agree nor disagree	agree	strongly agree

12. I have saved a considerable amount of money.

1	2	3	4	5
strongly disagree	disagree	neither agree nor disagree	agree	strongly agree

13. I earn more money than most of my friends.

1	2	3	4	5
strongly disagree	disagree	neither agree nor disagree	agree	strongly agree

14. I rarely think about money.

1	2	3	4	5
strongly disagree	disagree	neither agree nor disagree	agree	strongly agree

15. I can afford to buy most anything I want.

1	2	3	4	5
strongly disagree	disagree	neither agree nor disagree	agree	strongly agree

+ scoring

The first step is to reverse score items 1, 3, 4, 5, 7, 8, 9, 10, and 11. For these items, if you circled 5, change it to a 1, a 4 becomes a 2, a 3 remains a 3, a 2 becomes a 4, and a 1 becomes a 5.

This test consists of two scales, a Wealth scale and a Money Attitude scale. To find your Wealth score, add your points for items 1, 4, 7, and 10. To find your Money Attitudes score, add your points for items 2, 3, 5, 8, 9, 11, and 14. Items 6, 12, 13, and 15 are not scored. High scores on both scales suggest you have the requisite wealth and attitudes toward money that lead to happiness.

WEALTH SCORE	MONEY ATTITUDES SCORE	PERCENTILE
20	32	85
20	29	70
20	25	50
20	22	30
18	19	15

+ about the money test

The saying money can't buy happiness has achieved the status of cliché because it contains a grain of truth, a very large grain. Most of us, though, might be a little skeptical. Sure, we nod our heads in agreement when we hear this statement, but we cannot help but think that with a little more money, we could be a lot happier. We see people driving their luxury cars to their big houses overlooking the ocean, and we cannot help but think that if we were in their shoes, we would have an easy life. The truth is, we are firmly of two minds about it all. We readily agree that money can't buy happiness, but we also believe that money can solve a lot of problems and, without those problems, life would surely be more fun.

There has been considerable research conducted over the past decade regarding the link between wealth and happiness, and it turns out that there is some reason to have ambivalent feelings about this issue. It turns out that there is a relationship, albeit a modest relationship, between wealth and happiness. People in the top income groups tend to be somewhat happier than people in the middle income groups, who, in turn, are happier than those in the lowest income groups. But this relationship between wealth and happiness is very small. It was found, for instance, that the fabulously wealthy people in the *Forbes* 100 were only very slightly happier than average Americans.

An especially interesting area of research has looked at the average wealth of countries and the happiness of their citizens. University of Illinois psychologist Ed Diener and his colleagues examined the relationship between wealth and life satisfaction for forty countries and found a minor relationship. People in the poorest countries, such as Bulgaria and Romania, were indeed considerably less happy than people in the richer countries, such as Germany, Switzerland, and the United States. But it is interesting to note that once the wealth of a country reached a certain level (roughly, eight thousand dollars per capita), the link between wealth and happiness virtually disappeared. People in Ireland, for instance, are just as happy as U.S. citizens, even though their purchasing power is only half of ours. Diener's results also provide hints that some cultures may promote values that are associated with happiness. The Chinese, for example, were considerably happier than the Japanese, even though they had only one-tenth the purchasing power.

The consensus among the experts is that the relationship between wealth and happiness holds primarily for the very poor, those who cannot afford to provide the basic necessities for themselves. So, as the norms on the Wealth scale suggest, most everyone reading these words has more than enough money to be happy. If you have enough to eat, have a place to live, and are able to stay warm during the winter, you have all you need to be happy.

You might be surprised to learn (I know I was) that even the wretchedly poor are not necessarily unhappy. Robert Biswas-Diener, Ed Diener's son and an amateur scientist, traveled extensively to administer questionnaires to the residents of some of the world's least happy places, including prostitutes and pavement dwellers in Calcutta. He described in detail the life of one woman, Kalpana, who earned $2.50 per customer. She lived alone and practiced her profession in a small concrete room, furnished with the bare essentials. While she was dissatisfied with her income, she was as happy with her relationships with family and friends as were Calcutta University students. Biswas-Diener's research also revealed a variable that may be important regarding happiness among the poor—namely, one's comparison level. Among the very poor that he surveyed were street people of Fresno, California. These people were markedly un-happier than were the pavement dwellers of Calcutta, presumably because their poverty was made salient by living in the midst of relative wealth.

There are two more pieces of evidence that money cannot buy happiness. First, lottery winners are no happier six months after winning (and some are less happy) than they were before claiming their jackpot. Sure, they experienced a rush of exhilaration after discovering their win, but it gradually faded and they returned to their typical level of happiness. Second, the real income of Americans has doubled over the past fifty years, but we are not one bit happier than were our grandparents. I included items 6, 12, 13, and 15 to make this point. Having a sizable nest egg in the bank, earning more than your friends, and being able to buy most anything you want are irrelevant to your happiness.

Our attitudes toward money are much more relevant to our happiness than the money itself. If you received a low score on the Money Attitudes Test, you would have a better chance of increasing your happiness by changing your attitudes than by winning the lottery. The key is, I believe, our tendency to compare ourselves with those who have more than we do. Many of us are probably not that much different from the street people of Fresno. We see that others have nicer cars, larger houses, and fancier clothes than we do, and it leaves us feeling inadequate. Our feelings of inadequacy inspire us to compete with the proverbial Joneses, and we slowly dig a hole for ourselves that leaves us convinced that if only we had a little more money, we could be happy. To illustrate this point, consider item 5: "I never have enough money to pay all the bills at the end of the month." For most of us (the truly poor are an exception) the problem is not that we do not have enough money, but rather we spend more than we should in a futile attempt to buy happiness. Not only is this strategy destined to fail, it can actually reduce our happiness. I know one woman who paid ten thousand dollars for dining room furniture but then stopped inviting people over for dinner because she was so concerned that they might spill their drinks on her beautiful table. Two years after making the purchase that brought her so much initial satisfaction, she had drifted apart from several of her friends and was less happy than she was before buying something she had always wanted. As several of the items on the Money Attitude Test reflect, the key problem is envy. If we envy our friends who earn more money than we do or who live in bigger houses, we are bound to feel unhappy about our financial situation.

As I write about this issue, I cannot help but think of the wonderful book by Thomas Stanley and William Danko, *The Millionaire Next Door*. For those of you who have not read it, Stanley and Danko interviewed a sizable number of people who had a net worth of at least one million dollars and compared them to people who earned a great deal of money but who had failed to accumulate much wealth. As the title of their book suggests, the typical millionaire was much like your next-door neighbor. They were likely to buy used American-made cars rather than new, luxury imports, and they were more likely to wear a Timex than a Rolex. What they had in common was that they lived below their means and invested their extra money over a period of many years. My suspicion is that while feelings of inadequacy and the envy it inspires can cause people to go into debt, a sense of self-worth, a quiet confidence that personal values are what is truly important may very well lead to financial wealth. For those of you who received low scores on the Money Attitudes Test, I am confident that if you learn to live below your means you will be happier, and I strongly suspect you will become wealthier as well.

will your goals lead you to happiness?

The following phrases describe people's behaviors, attitudes, and feelings. Indicate the extent to which you agree that the statement describes you.

1. I have a clear idea of what I want to achieve in my life.

1	2	3	4	5
strongly disagree	disagree	neither agree nor disagree	agree	strongly agree

2. I have developed a strategy for accomplishing my goals.

1	2	3	4	5
strongly disagree	disagree	neither agree nor disagree	agree	strongly agree

3. I have researched the requirements for reaching my goals.

1	2	3	4	5
strongly disagree	disagree	neither agree nor disagree	agree	strongly agree

4. I worry that I may fail to accomplish my goals.

1	2	3	4	5
strongly disagree	disagree	neither agree nor disagree	agree	strongly agree

5. I am willing to work hard to accomplish my goals.

1	2	3	4	5
strongly disagree	disagree	neither agree nor disagree	agree	strongly agree

6. I understand my motives for selecting the goals I have.

1	2	3	4	5
strongly disagree	disagree	neither agree nor disagree	agree	strongly agree

7. I am a persistent person.

1	2	3	4	5
strongly disagree	disagree	neither agree nor disagree	agree	strongly agree

8. I enjoy learning new things.

1	2	3	4	5
strongly disagree	disagree	neither agree nor disagree	agree	strongly agree

9. I am willing to sacrifice a little fun in the short-term in order to work toward my long-term goals.

1	2	3	4	5
strongly disagree	disagree	neither agree nor disagree	agree	strongly agree

10. I worry that others may see my goals as too ambitious.

1	2	3	4	5
strongly disagree	disagree	neither agree nor disagree	agree	strongly agree

11. When I get involved with a project, I read as much as I can about it.

1	2	3	4	5
strongly disagree	disagree	neither agree nor disagree	agree	strongly agree

12. I have confidence that I can do what it takes to accomplish my goals.

1	2	3	4	5
strongly disagree	disagree	neither agree nor disagree	agree	strongly agree

13. I am able to objectively analyze my strengths.

1	2	3	4	5
strongly disagree	disagree	neither agree nor disagree	agree	strongly agree

14. I am willing to acknowledge my limitations.

1	2	3	4	5
strongly disagree	disagree	neither agree nor disagree	agree	strongly agree

15. I feel more strongly about my values than do most people.

1	2	3	4	5
strongly disagree	disagree	neither agree nor disagree	agree	strongly agree

+ scoring

The first step is to reverse score items 4 and 10. For these items, if you circled 5, change it to a 1, a 4 becomes a 2, a 3 remains a 3, a 2 becomes a 4, and a 1 becomes a 5. After you have made these changes, add your points together for your total score on the Goals Test. High scores indicate a high ability to set goals that will increase your chances of happiness.

GOALS SCORE	PERCENTILE
61	85
57	70
52	50
47	30
43	15

+ about the goals test

During my undergraduate years I, like most college students, thoroughly enjoyed those late-night discussions on what life was all about. Even then my beliefs did not quite fit the mainstream, and many of my friends accused me of being hedonistic and superficial because my position was that happiness should be our ultimate goal. This was back in the late 1960s when our cities were burning and hundreds of young men were dying each week in a war we couldn't understand, and it was thus difficult to convince my friends that my philosophy was not as shallow as it may have appeared. Now, nearly forty years after my failure to make a convincing argument, University of Maryland psychologist Edwin Locke has articulated my beliefs much better than I was ever able to. He wrote, "One's highest moral purpose is the achievement of one's happiness." And he believes the best way to do that, as I did as a college student and still do today, is by understanding the values that are important to us and setting goals that reflect those values.

Locke wrote that we all have an ever-shifting mixture of values, but most fundamental are our moral values, deciding what is good and bad, right and wrong. These broad, fundamental values will influence our specific, or rational, values. Rational values help us fulfill our needs, both physical and psychological. We may value education, for instance, because we believe it will satisfy our need for self-esteem as well as our need to earn enough money for food and shelter. Rational values are likely to change over the course of our lives. When we are young adults, we may value education and love relationships. A few years down the road, we may value competence in our job and teaching our children appropriate values. In our later years, spending time with grandchildren and friends may be high on our list of priorities.

Locke provided a detailed strategy for setting goals, and because space does not permit a full presentation of his views, I'll discuss a few of his ideas that seem especially important. First, we must set our goals high because the higher our goals, the greater our accomplishments are likely to be. I see the importance of this every day in college students, presumably people who all value education. I have known countless students with modest natural abilities but with very high goals who performed at a much higher level than students with more ability but who had the rather modest goal of simply graduating. Second, specific goals are more likely to be effective than vague, general goals. The student whose goal is to receive a ninety-five on the final exam is likely to do better than the student whose goal is to do well or to give it his or her best effort. Third, and to my mind the most significant element, is commitment to one's goals. When we set difficult and specific goals, it requires a great deal of effort to reach them. Commitment is likely to be enhanced, according to Locke, when we believe the goal is important and when we believe that it is attainable. This last point can be a little tricky since our goals must be difficult but not so difficult that they are impossible for us to achieve.

It may seem as if Locke's goal-oriented strategy for finding happiness applies only to areas in which we strive to achieve, but he has described how this approach can be used to find romantic love as well. His basic premise is that romantic relationships involve trade, much as business relationships do. But unlike business in which we trade products or services for money, in romantic relationships we trade our character for our potential partner's character. So, if our goal is to find love, especially a love that is likely to last, our task is to become more lovable, to develop character. Character might include having direction in our life, having passion for what we do, or behaving with maturity and respect for others. Once we become lovable, we must articulate our goals for what we want in a partner, and most of us would like a partner with character traits similar to our own. Locke acknowledges that specific goals may not be of much use in the early stages of a relationship. After all, romantic love is about emotions, about that almost mystical connection we feel for another human being. But by having clear goals for love, we are likely to be happier in the long run. Who among us has not felt an intense attraction for someone we knew would make us miserable a few years down the road? If we have clear goals for love, we may have the strength to make a rational decision to ignore our feelings and terminate the relationship.

Locke has observed that most people seem to have an intuitive understanding that setting goals, that having a purposefulness to our lives, is critical to having a successful and happy life. Why, then, he asks, are so many people unhappy? He offered three explanations. The first, and most important, he believes, is irrationality. As we mentioned above, this often happens in love relationships. The woman who says, "He'll stop drinking so much once he settles down," or the man who believes, "She'll be less volatile once we are married," are being irrational, and at some level, they know it.

A second reason that many people fail to utilize goal setting effectively is that they are unwilling to put forth either the mental or physical effort. My colleagues and I talk about this all the time, and while it may be a sign that we are all becoming a bunch of old fogies, we wonder why so many students are unwilling to make an effort to do well in their classes. If the weather is nice on a Friday, perhaps half of the students will attend a large lecture class despite the clear evidence that attendance is one of the best predictors of grades.

Finally, Locke believes that our fears interfere with our ability to pursue our goals. We fail to approach potential love partners because we fear rejection, we do not share our feelings with those close to us because we fear ridicule, and we do not sit down to write that great American novel because we fear failure.

I firmly believe that those of you who received low scores on the Goals Test can be happier if you follow Locke's advice and set specific goals that reflect your values and make the commitment to work toward those goals. I would, however, add one additional thought. In my experience it is more effective to set goals that involve actions you can actually control than it is to set goals that reflect outcomes. To use what might seem to be a trivial example (but one that is important to me), it would do me little good to set a goal of shooting seventy-five on the golf course. Simply having such a lofty goal would probably do little to make me a better golfer. I would be more likely to improve my game if I set goals such as hitting ten consecutive shots onto the green during my practice session. I have limited control over my final score on the course, but I have considerable control over my behavior during a practice session. Similarly, an insurance salesman might set a goal of calling ten prospects every day as opposed to the goal of selling five policies a week. I tell my clients that as long as they are persistent in meeting the goals they can control, the desired results are likely to follow. The same is true for you.

personal life

+ + +

is your glass half full?

The following phrases describe people's behaviors, attitudes, and feelings. Indicate the extent to which you agree that the statement describes you.

1. When I face a new situation, I usually expect the best.

1	2	3	4	5
strongly disagree	disagree	neither agree nor disagree	agree	strongly agree

2. If I have to deal with a problem, it usually turns out badly for me.

1	2	3	4	5
strongly disagree	disagree	neither agree nor disagree	agree	strongly agree

3. I always think my future looks bright.

1	2	3	4	5
strongly disagree	disagree	neither agree nor disagree	agree	strongly agree

4. Things rarely turn out the way I would like them to.

1	2	3	4	5
strongly disagree	disagree	neither agree nor disagree	agree	strongly agree

5. I cannot remember anything good happening to me unexpectedly.

1	2	3	4	5
strongly disagree	disagree	neither agree nor disagree	agree	strongly agree

6. When I start a new project, I expect to succeed at it.

1	2	3	4	5
strongly disagree	disagree	neither agree nor disagree	agree	strongly agree

7. I have many good friends I can count on.

1	2	3	4	5
strongly disagree	disagree	neither agree nor disagree	agree	strongly agree

8. When I plan carefully, I know things will turn out fine.

1	2	3	4	5
strongly disagree	disagree	neither agree nor disagree	agree	strongly agree

9. If I count on others too much, I usually end up disappointed.

1	2	3	4	5
strongly disagree	disagree	neither agree nor disagree	agree	strongly agree

10. Much of my life has been disappointing.

1	2	3	4	5
strongly disagree	disagree	neither agree nor disagree	agree	strongly agree

11. I think of myself as an optimistic person.

1	2	3	4	5
strongly disagree	disagree	neither agree nor disagree	agree	strongly agree

12. I sometimes make a mountain out of a molehill.

1	2	3	4	5
strongly disagree	disagree	neither agree nor disagree	agree	strongly agree

13. When I am faced with a new project, all I can see are obstacles.

1	2	3	4	5
strongly disagree	disagree	neither agree nor disagree	agree	strongly agree

14. I believe I can accomplish most anything I want to.

1	2	3	4	5
strongly disagree	disagree	neither agree nor disagree	agree	strongly agree

15. Life is filled with disappointments.

1	2	3	4	5
strongly disagree	disagree	neither agree nor disagree	agree	strongly agree

+ scoring

The first step is to reverse score items 2, 4, 5, 9, 10, 12, 13, and 15. For these items, if you circled 5 change it to a 1, a 4 becomes a 2, a 3 remains a 3, a 2 becomes a 4, and a 1 becomes a 5. After you have made these changes, add your points together for your total score on the Optimism Test. High scores indicate a high level of optimism.

OPTIMISM SCORE	PERCENTILE
48	**85**
43	70
35	**50**
27	30
22	**15**

+ about the optimism test

When I was home for a visit during my second year of graduate school, I told my mother about what I was learning in my psychotherapy courses. She listened attentively before commenting, "A positive attitude makes all the difference in the world." I was annoyed with my mom because I thought she was oversimplifying what I was telling her, but guess what? After thirty years of research, it seems that she was right.

For more than twenty years, researchers have been using tests very similar to the one you just completed to document the beneficial effects of optimism. Optimism can result in better performance at work, it can ward off depression when things do go wrong, it helps people adjust to life transitions, and it is even related to better physical health. A positive attitude really does seem to make all the difference in the world.

A critical difference between optimists and pessimists lies in the coping strategies they use when faced with challenges. Optimists tend to approach such challenges with a problem-solving focus. They want to understand the situation, and they search for appropriate solutions. If they are presented with a challenge for which there is no good solution, they tend to use what psychologists have called adaptive emotion-focused coping strategies. This is a fancy way of saying that optimists try to see the bright side of bad situations. They may view it as a learning experience or use humor to defuse the situation, decreasing the odds that they will make the same mistake twice. Pessimists, on the other hand, are likely to feel helpless in the face of challenges and react with more negative emotions. They see unfortunate events as confirming their negative view of the world. If you scored below the 30th percentile, you may want to work on making changes in your outlook on life.

It is never easy to change a characteristic that may seem so basic to our personality. The glass-is-half-empty view of the world usually begins quite early in life and becomes deeply ingrained as we grow older. But there is abundant evidence that these attitudes can be changed with sufficient effort and persistence. The first step, obviously, is for you to make the decision that this is something about yourself that you want to change. Keep in mind that shifting to an optimistic position may not only increase the happiness and joy you experience but is likely to help you live a longer, healthier life.

Once you have decided to try to adopt a more optimistic view of the world, you must begin by identifying your pessimistic thoughts, though this may be difficult. Roger, for instance, was a first-year graduate student who came to me for therapy after receiving a failing grade in one of his courses. He was convinced that his poor grade portended a host of bad things that would happen to him in the immediate future. When I pressed him as to why he believed this, he responded, "Because nothing good ever happens to me." I briefly reviewed his history with him. A few years earlier he had graduated cum laude from a good university, he taught high school successfully for four years, he married a woman he loved, and had a healthy baby boy. And once he decided to return to graduate school, he was accepted to his first choice of programs. He reluctantly agreed that more good things had happened to him than bad and that perhaps his pessimism was not grounded in reality.

Like Roger, you may have difficulty in identifying your own pessimistic beliefs. To you they may seem to reflect reality. If so, a good place to begin is with the items on the optimism test. Do you expect the worst during uncertain times? Do you believe that if something can go wrong, it will? Make a list of your pessimistic beliefs and after you are finished, show it to your spouse, a close friend, or even a parent. He or she may be able to add a few more of your pessimistic beliefs to the list and, as a bonus, is likely to offer support and guidance. Sometimes others know us better than we know ourselves.

Once you have become familiar with your gloomy thoughts, you must make an effort to put them out of your mind and replace them with positive, optimistic thoughts. Therapists who specialize in cognitive behavior therapy have developed techniques to make this possible. These techniques are based on the premise that thoughts are habits that have much in common with behavioral habits such as biting one's fingernails. Bad thought habits can be changed just as bad behavioral habits can, with effort and persistence. The first step is called thought stopping. This requires that you be diligent in identifying your pessimistic thoughts. Once one of these thoughts pops into your mind, you must do something to rid yourself of it. If you are alone, you might slam your hand on your desk and yell stop. If you are around other people, yell stop in your mind. Some therapists recommend a rubber band technique. This requires you to wear a heavy-gauge rubber band around your wrist and when you have a pessimistic thought, give yourself a little pop. The mild pain serves to interrupt the sequence of your thoughts that has become automatic for you.

After interrupting your pessimistic thought, replace it with an optimistic one. Gwen, for example, was a chronic pessimist who believed that anything out of her usual routine was a sign that something bad was about to happen. Several times per week her supervisor would call to ask her to come to her office and invariably Gwen would conclude that she had done something wrong and would be reprimanded. Even though this almost never happened and, when it did, the rebukes were more like reminders, nonetheless, Gwen's stomach would be in knots during the twenty to thirty minutes she was waiting to speak to her supervisor. Gwen used the rubber band to interrupt her pessimistic thoughts and then told herself, "She simply wants to talk about the situation with my current client." This process felt artificial and strained to her for several weeks but after two months, it began to feel more comfortable and natural.

I'm not sure that Gwen ever came to see the glass as being more than half full, but she did approach the 50th percentile on the Optimism Test. At the very least, she no longer became tense with anxiety every time her supervisor called. And once she could approach her supervisor in a more relaxed way, they learned they had much in common and began to have lunch together on occasion.

An especially intriguing implication of optimism is that it is related to a longer and healthier life. Researchers have yet to unravel exactly why this is, but we do know that optimistic people respond to certain situations differently from their pessimistic cousins. It has been found, for instance, that optimists have a better response to surgery than pessimists. Perhaps this is because they are more likely to follow the doctor's orders, they take seriously recommendations regarding exercise and diet, and they agree to eliminate bad habits such as smoking and drinking too much. They sincerely believe that if they do these things, they can live longer and have a higher quality of life. Pessimists, on the other hand, cannot see beyond their current situation. They seem to tell themselves, "I have a serious medical problem and there is nothing I can do to change my lot in life."

One last thought. Having an optimistic outlook does not always reflect the reality of our lives, but it almost always shapes the reality of our future. I know a woman who suffered a serious illness when she was twenty-five years old that left one of her legs paralyzed, leaving her confined to a wheelchair in her later years. After a year of intense fear about the future and extensive rehabilitation, she decided that she had to adopt a positive attitude about her life. She owed it to her young children if not to herself. Now, more than half a century later, this woman expresses amazement at how wonderful her life has been. She takes more pleasure in her friends and her family (especially her grandchildren) than anyone I know. This woman is my mom, the woman who told me thirty years ago that a positive outlook can make all the difference. She is so right.

how much do you trust others?

The following phrases describe people's behaviors, attitudes, and feelings. Indicate the extent to which you agree that the statement describes you.

1. I wonder if people really mean it when they say nice things about me.

1	2	3	4	5
strongly disagree	disagree	neither agree nor disagree	agree	strongly agree

2. I can confide in my friends and know that they will not tell others what I said.

1	2	3	4	5
strongly disagree	disagree	neither agree nor disagree	agree	strongly agree

3. If my alarm clock were broken and I asked one of my friends to call me to wake me up for an important meeting, I would have confidence that I would get the call.

1	2	3	4	5
strongly disagree	disagree	neither agree nor disagree	agree	strongly agree

4. I would lend my car to my friends.

1	2	3	4	5
strongly disagree	disagree	neither agree nor disagree	agree	strongly agree

5. When I hire a repair person, I believe I will be treated fairly most of the time.

1	2	3	4	5
strongly disagree	disagree	neither agree nor disagree	agree	strongly agree

6. When my friends promise me a favor, I can count on them to follow through.

1	2	3	4	5
strongly disagree	disagree	neither agree nor disagree	agree	strongly agree

7. My colleagues would never say anything to harm my reputation at work.

1	2	3	4	5
strongly disagree	disagree	neither agree nor disagree	agree	strongly agree

8. It is better not to trust others until they have earned your trust.

1	2	3	4	5
strongly disagree	disagree	neither agree nor disagree	agree	strongly agree

9. Most salespeople will lie in order to make the sale.

1	2	3	4	5
strongly disagree	disagree	neither agree nor disagree	agree	strongly agree

10. Other people will take advantage of you if you give them the chance.

1	2	3	4	5
strongly disagree	disagree	neither agree nor disagree	agree	strongly agree

11. I can count on my spouse or partner to always have my best interests in mind.

1	2	3	4	5
strongly disagree	disagree	neither agree nor disagree	agree	strongly agree

12. You can count on most people to tell the truth.

1	2	3	4	5
strongly disagree	disagree	neither agree nor disagree	agree	strongly agree

13. When I leave my pet with a friend, I do not have to worry that it will be taken good care of.

1	2	3	4	5
strongly disagree	disagree	neither agree nor disagree	agree	strongly agree

14. It is better to be skeptical about the motives of others.

1	2	3	4	5
strongly disagree	disagree	neither agree nor disagree	agree	strongly agree

15. I can trust my family to make medical decisions for me should it become necessary.

1	2	3	4	5
strongly disagree	disagree	neither agree nor disagree	agree	strongly agree

+ scoring

The first step is to reverse score items 8, 9, 10, and 14. For these items, if you circled 5, change it to a 1, a 4 becomes a 2, a 3 remains a 3, a 2 becomes a 4, and a 1 becomes a 5. After you have made these changes, add your points together for your total score on the Trust Test. High scores indicate a high level of trust.

TRUST SCORE	PERCENTILE
54	**85**
48	70
44	**50**
40	30
36	**15**

+ about the trust test

Without trust, our day-to-day existence would be extremely difficult. We trust that drivers will stop for red lights, we trust that the food we buy in the grocery store is safe and nutritious, we trust schools to educate and safeguard our children, and we trust our physician to competently diagnose and treat our medical problems. Even the most ordinary social and business interactions would be fraught with difficulty without trust. Even the most suspicious and cynical among us are capable of at least some trust, but if you scored below the 30th percentile on the Trust Test, you have the potential to be happier by learning to increase your trust in others. There may be more at stake than your happiness. John Barefoot and his colleagues at the Duke University Medical Center found that not only was trust related to life satisfaction but it was also related to longevity. They measured trust in one hundred men and women between the ages of fifty-five and eighty and discovered that those with high scores on a measure of trust had higher levels of life satisfaction. When they contacted these people again fourteen years later, they found that the men and women who were initially low in trust were more likely to be deceased. It is not clear why this relationship exists, but, though additional research is needed to confirm the link, the possibility of a happier, longer life is good reason to learn to trust.

Psychologist Michael Gurtman of the University of Wisconsin has conducted one of the more comprehensive studies on the relationship between trust and interpersonal problems. He found that people who scored high on a measure of trust consistently had fewer problems than those less capable of trusting others. This is not to say that people who trust others never have problems, but it does indicate that high levels of trust do seem to serve a protective function. Trust makes it less likely that one will experience a great deal of distress on a day-to-day basis. People low in trust, on the other hand, consistently reported a variety of problems. These men and women were found to have problems with competitiveness, envy, resentfulness, vindictiveness, and lack of feeling for others. An overall theme associated with low trust was hostility, which makes sense. If you do not trust your car mechanic to be honest with you about the cost of repairs or if you cannot trust your supervisor to evaluate your work in a fair and objective way, it would not be surprising for you to feel angry and resentful much of the time.

Some of the specific beliefs expressed by those with low levels of trust in Gurtman's research were surprising. While we would expect these people to admit that they are too suspicious of other people and feel attacked by other people too much, they also report beliefs that they are overly generous to other people and trust other people too much. It is curious how one could believe that he or she is both too suspicious and too trusting, but it seems to reflect a person who feels a great deal of disappointment in his or her relationships. I would guess that these people do not trust others as much as they claim and that their suspiciousness leads them to conclude that any trust is too much. If we expect the worst from others, we are likely to find it.

A few years ago I was having a conversation with a relative about car repairs. We both recently had safety inspections for our cars and we both had to make about two hundred dollars' worth of repairs before we could get our sticker. My relative was convinced that she was cheated and that mechanics regularly cheated all women. I asked her why I had to pay two hundred dollars as well and why the mechanic would cheat me? She thought about it for a while and then with a flash of insight came up with the answer, "Because you are a college professor. He knows you don't know anything about cars." When I tried to convince her that the repairs were most likely necessary (after all, our cars had more than a few years on them), she accused me of being naive. I let the argument drop in the interest of family harmony, but I could have cited scientific research that suggests she was wrong. Eminent psychologist Julian Rotter, who initiated interest and research in this topic twenty-five years ago, considered the possibility that extreme trust would result in gullibility or naïveté. But he found that this was not the case, that people high in trust were not necessarily foolish. Once betrayed by a person, high trusters are no more likely to behave gullibly than low trusters. It seems that those high in trust take the position that they will trust others until they have reason not to. Those low in trust approach all interactions from a position of suspiciousness.

It can be difficult for suspicious, cynical people to learn to trust others, and most theorists believe that the origins of distrust lie in the childhood years. Many distrustful people had parents who failed to care for them adequately or may have abandoned or abused them. They learned at an early age that you cannot count on others to satisfy your needs or even to be there for you. Distrust is usually a deeply engrained and pervasive way of viewing the world, and there are countless articles in the scientific literature that suggest that lengthy, intensive psychotherapy is required to help these people learn to trust. While a competent therapist would certainly help people regain a sense of trust, I do believe it is possible for many people to make progress on their own using cognitive techniques. The most important step is to accept the proposition that the best policy is to trust others until they give you reason to distrust them. Remember, this does not mean that you have to become gullible or foolish, but it is important for your own happiness and peace of mind to accept the idea that most people have good intentions and will treat you fairly. Let me give you an example. My relative's suspiciousness extends to physicians. She is convinced that they prescribe unnecessary procedures to increase their profits, so she approaches every appointment with her temper just below the boiling point. On those occasions when she has been told that some procedure is necessary, she has made her feelings clear and announced her intentions to get a second opinion.

There is nothing wrong with getting a second opinion; indeed, it is often the smart thing to do. And yes, there are physicians who perform unnecessary operations for the money. But the chances are high that her physician's intentions were good even if his diagnosis turned out to be wrong. So rather than making angry accusations, she could have said something like, "I'm sure you can understand that this is a very big decision for me, so I hope you won't mind if I get a second opinion." By treating her physician with respect and courtesy and by trusting him, she is more likely to receive the sort of treatment she expects than if she angrily accuses him of dishonesty or incompetence. And she will feel happier as well.

+ 12 +

are you a sociable person?

The following phrases describe people's behaviors, attitudes, and feelings. Indicate the extent to which you agree that the statement describes you.

1. I tend to keep my distance from other people.

1	2	3	4	5
strongly disagree	disagree	neither agree nor disagree	agree	strongly agree

2. At parties, I talk to lots of different people.

1	2	3	4	5
strongly disagree	disagree	neither agree nor disagree	agree	strongly agree

3. I feel comfortable when I am around other people.

1	2	3	4	5
strongly disagree	disagree	neither agree nor disagree	agree	strongly agree

4. I sometimes feel lost when I am in a group of people.

1	2	3	4	5
strongly disagree	disagree	neither agree nor disagree	agree	strongly agree

5. I like to get others involved in what I am doing.

1	2	3	4	5
strongly disagree	disagree	neither agree nor disagree	agree	strongly agree

6. Other people see me as a cheerful person.

1	2	3	4	5
strongly disagree	disagree	neither agree nor disagree	agree	strongly agree

7. It is easy for me to make new friends.

1	2	3	4	5
strongly disagree	disagree	neither agree nor disagree	agree	strongly agree

8. I look forward to large parties.

1	2	3	4	5
strongly disagree	disagree	neither agree nor disagree	agree	strongly agree

9. It is easy to make me laugh.

1	2	3	4	5
strongly disagree	disagree	neither agree nor disagree	agree	strongly agree

10. It takes others a long time to get to know me well.

1	2	3	4	5
strongly disagree	disagree	neither agree nor disagree	agree	strongly agree

11. I would feel uncomfortable if my friends or family gave me a surprise party.

1	2	3	4	5
strongly disagree	disagree	neither agree nor disagree	agree	strongly agree

12. I can always see the bright side of things.

1	2	3	4	5
strongly disagree	disagree	neither agree nor disagree	agree	strongly agree

13. I am something of a loner.

1	2	3	4	5
strongly disagree	disagree	neither agree nor disagree	agree	strongly agree

14. Most people are interesting if you take the time to get to know them.

1	2	3	4	5
strongly disagree	disagree	neither agree nor disagree	agree	strongly agree

15. I would be annoyed if a friend dropped by without calling first.

1	2	3	4	5
strongly disagree	disagree	neither agree nor disagree	agree	strongly agree

+ scoring

The first step is to reverse score items 1, 4, 10, 11, 13, and 15. For these items, if you circled 5, change it to a 1, a 4 becomes a 2, a 3 remains a 3, a 2 becomes a 4, and a 1 becomes a 5. After you have made these changes, add your points together for your total score on the Sociability Test. High scores indicate a high level of sociability.

SOCIABILITY SCORE	PERCENTILE
53	85
49	70
44	50
39	30
35	15

+ about the sociability test

Psychological research has made it clear that there is a strong relationship between a person's level of extraversion and his or her happiness. This finding, that extraverted people are happier than their introverted peers, has been so widespread and so consistent that psychologist Leslie Francis of Trinity College titled her article in which she reported such results, "Happiness Is a Thing Called Stable Extraversion." This relationship between extraversion and happiness appears to apply to countries as well as individuals. University of Minnesota psychologists Steel Piers and Deniz Ones examined the average level of extraversion as well as the average level of happiness for citizens of fifteen different countries and found a substantial relationship. Countries in which people are more extraverted have happier citizens than those countries populated with introverts. Indeed, this relationship appears to be so robust that some researchers have wondered if it is possible for introverts to be happy. To my relief (I score somewhat below average on measures of extraversion), the answer is yes. There are indeed happy introverts, although they are not as common as happy extraverts.

One question that researchers have yet to answer is what it is about extraversion that leads to happiness. My guess is that sociability is the key. Extraverts do tend to be more sociable than introverts, but it is certainly possible for introverts to be sociable. They may do it in quieter, more subtle ways, but we have all known friendly, cheerful introverts who are interesting to talk with. But these people typically get low scores on measures of extraversion because such scales also include items that measure the desire to have new and exciting experiences—an important component of extraversion. This is why I have included the Sociability Test rather than a measure of extraversion.

I believe that sociability is the critical component of extraversion that results in greater happiness. As we have discussed in several places already, happy people have good relationships with others, they feel connected, they are involved, and they are sociable. If you did have a low score on this scale, do not despair. It is possible for you to change the way you interact with others.

In one of the more interesting studies I have read in some time, Wake Forest researcher William Fleeson and his colleagues instructed introverted people to act more outgoing in a group discussion and found that when they did so, they felt happier than when they assumed their usual quiet, reserved role. Especially fascinating was the researchers' finding that when extraverts were instructed to behave in a quiet, reserved manner during the group discussion, they felt less happy. The research participants' usual level of sociability did not seem to matter; everyone who acted outgoing and sociable was happier than when they acted quiet and reserved. As this research suggests, one need not be naturally extraverted or even sociable to be happy—one only needs to pretend to be.

Of course it would be a struggle to go through life pretending to be outgoing, though the good thing about pretending is that, before long, it becomes a habit. Ying's story is a good example of this phenomenon. She was a quiet and timid child, but during her adolescent years she became determined to change. It had become obvious to her that more sociable people not only seemed to be happier than she was but seemed to get more recognition from their teachers, coaches, and even from their peers. She began by studying her classmates who were especially sociable and who seemed to find it easy to talk with others. She noticed that they smiled often and laughed easily, were interested in other people, and always had something to say when they sat down next to someone at the beginning of class or bumped into a friend in the hallway. Ying began slowly. She practiced her pleasant smile in front of a mirror. She made a point of regularly offering friendly comments to classmates. She forced herself to participate in class discussions. And, hardest of all, she joined in the discussion when she was with a large group of people. Ying almost gave up those first few days. Her stomach was in knots much of the time, and she was on the verge of panic that others would view her changes as odd and question her about them. But the changes were much more dramatic to Ying than to her friends, and they responded well to her newfound sociability. They were more likely to go out of their way to talk with her, and they seemed to appreciate her subtle wit. Within a month, Ying learned that her teachers also were responding to her new persona. Although she was not studying any more than before, there was a noticeable increase in her grades.

When Ying discusses her personality makeover, she says that it took nearly a year for the changes to feel comfortable. And when she began high school, she experienced a tendency to revert to her quiet, reserved self, so she had to consciously reassert her more sociable side. She had similar experiences when she began college and when she accepted her first professional position. But now, twenty years later, she is completely comfortable with her role, and it has paid rich dividends. She has a large circle of friends and has been extraordinarily successful in her career. Ying is quick to say that her decision to change her personality during middle school had a profound effect on her life.

It is true that there is a genetic component to extraversion or sociability. Some people are born to be outgoing and friendly, while others are born to be timid and reserved. But research has also found that our genetic predisposition is not necessarily our destiny. While it may seem unfair to those of us who are naturally shy that being part of the crowd comes so easily for others, our inborn reticence does not mean that we are foreordained to have lonely, isolated, and unhappy lives. We can pretend to be outgoing and sociable, and if we are persistent about it, like Ying, these changes will become a part of us.

I also suspect that there are some advantages to being naturally shy. I think it makes people more sensitive to others and less likely to have a need to be the center of attention. We have all known outgoing people who simply overdo it. They always have something to say and they would much rather do the talking than the listening. Some naturally extraverted people can be obnoxious jerks, something that naturally shy people are rarely accused of. Shy people who have learned to be sociable make delightful friends and romantic partners. They are genuinely interested in others, and this makes others feel they are interesting people. Because they are less inclined to dominate relationships, sociable shys have an ability to make others feel comfortable, even important. Sociable shys often bring out the best in those around them. So if you did receive a low score on the Sociability Test, think of it as an advantage. Once you learn to be sociable, you will have much to offer to those around you.

+ 13 +

do you control your own fate?

The following phrases describe people's behaviors, attitudes, and feelings. Indicate the extent to which you agree that the statement describes you.

1. Most people with unhappy lives are the victims of bad luck.

1	2	3	4	5
strongly disagree	disagree	neither agree nor disagree	agree	strongly agree

2. People who work hard generally get the respect they deserve.

1	2	3	4	5
strongly disagree	disagree	neither agree nor disagree	agree	strongly agree

3. Having a successful marriage is mostly a matter of luck.

1	2	3	4	5
strongly disagree	disagree	neither agree nor disagree	agree	strongly agree

4. Well-prepared students rarely complain that a test was unfair.

1	2	3	4	5
strongly disagree	disagree	neither agree nor disagree	agree	strongly agree

5. When I make plans, I am confident that I can make them work.

1	2	3	4	5
strongly disagree	disagree	neither agree nor disagree	agree	strongly agree

6. To be successful, one has to get the right breaks.

1	2	3	4	5
strongly disagree	disagree	neither agree nor disagree	agree	strongly agree

7. If more people took the time to vote, our government would be better.

1	2	3	4	5
strongly disagree	disagree	neither agree nor disagree	agree	strongly agree

8. Success is mostly a matter of hard work.

1	2	3	4	5
strongly disagree	disagree	neither agree nor disagree	agree	strongly agree

9. No matter what you do, some people just won't like you.

1	2	3	4	5
strongly disagree	disagree	neither agree nor disagree	agree	strongly agree

10. I am responsible for what happens to me.

1	2	3	4	5
strongly disagree	disagree	neither agree nor disagree	agree	strongly agree

11. People don't have as much control over their lives as they like to think.

1	2	3	4	5
strongly disagree	disagree	neither agree nor disagree	agree	strongly agree

12. Students who finish at the top of their class have had a lot of luck along the way.

1	2	3	4	5
strongly disagree	disagree	neither agree nor disagree	agree	strongly agree

13. There will always be wars no matter what people do.

1	2	3	4	5
strongly disagree	disagree	neither agree nor disagree	agree	strongly agree

14. If I get what I want, luck won't have much to do with it.

1	2	3	4	5
strongly disagree	disagree	neither agree nor disagree	agree	strongly agree

15. If I were to fail, it would be my own fault.

1	2	3	4	5
strongly disagree	disagree	neither agree nor disagree	agree	strongly agree

+ scoring

The first step is to reverse score items 1, 3, 6, 9, 11, 12, and 13. For these items, if you circled 5, change it to a 1, a 4 becomes a 2, a 3 remains a 3, a 2 becomes a 4, and a 1 becomes a 5. After you have made these changes, add your points together for your total score on the Internal Locus of Control Test. High scores indicate a high degree of internal locus of control.

INTERNAL LOCUS OF CONTROL SCORE	PERCENTILE
53	85
49	70
44	50
39	30
35	15

+ about the internal locus of control test

Nearly half a century ago, the eminent psychologist Julian Rotter developed the first test to measure locus of control. Since that time there have been hundreds of studies that demonstrated that people who score high on the such tests have a number of desirable characteristics relative to low scorers, not the least of which is greater happiness. As you can tell from the items on this test, the personality dimension of locus of control refers to our views about what determines our fate. Those with an internal locus of control believe that they are masters of their destiny, that their efforts make a difference. They tend to dismiss the role of luck and chance and believe that people get pretty much what they deserve. Those with low scores, those with an external locus of control, tend to believe that their own efforts do not matter much, that they are powerless to exert an influence over the direction of their lives. If you received a low score on this scale, developing an internal locus of control might help you increase the odds that you will accomplish your goals as well as helping you to feel more satisfied with your life.

Our locus of control results from our experiences. Most people with low scores on this scale had parents who would also score low. Their parents took the position that our own efforts do not matter much, that forces beyond our control shape our destiny. Frank's father was one of these people. He hated his job on an assembly line in a factory, and his bitterness at never improving his lot in life often spilled over at the dinner table. He would blame others, the owners and managers of the factory, for never giving him a chance to move up in the world. "You have to know the right people," Frank remembers his father saying with some frequency, "if you're going to get ahead in this world." By the time Frank began high school, he had little hope of having a life different from that of his unhappy parents because there was little chance of meeting the right people in his neighborhood.

Nina also learned to have an external locus of control, although the message she received from her parents was somewhat different. Like Frank's, Nina's parents were dissatisfied with their lives but they believed their bad luck was to blame. Whenever a neighbor or relative acquired some sign of success, such as a new car or house, her mother and father would wonder aloud, "How did they get so lucky?" Nina's mother placed her hopes for a more satisfying life on winning the lottery, while her father was always on the lookout for just the right get-rich-quick scheme. They often wondered when their luck would change. People with an external locus of control cannot accept the premise that their own efforts make a difference. They are convinced that their lives are ruled either by luck or by powerful others.

This inability to appreciate the role of one's efforts results in a sense of futility and helplessness. Students with an external locus of control wonder why they should bother studying when so many professors give unfair tests. Employees with this orientation see little point in working hard when their success depends largely on getting the right breaks. It comes as no surprise that low scorers are more susceptible to depression and less capable of overcoming their depression once it sets in.

There is evidence that psychotherapy, self-help books, and even life experiences can modify one's locus of control. Sometimes it can happen quite suddenly and unexpectedly, as it did in Frank's case. He longed for a life different from his father's but he was convinced that he would have little chance to get it. After all, his family did not have the money for college and you had to know someone to get into the best colleges anyway. Frank experienced an epiphany during his sophomore year in high school when his homeroom teacher talked about college planning. Frank had never heard about college loans or work-study programs. And he was amazed when his teacher told him that with his test scores and grades he had a good chance of earning a scholarship. Frank left school that day with a sense of determination to take control of his future and vague feelings of anger at his father for making excuses and failing to do anything about his lot if life except complain.

In most cases, changing one's locus of control takes more persistence and sometimes help from others. Nina, for instance, was directionless by the time she reached her mid-twenties. She had failed out of college twice and had a series of minimum-wage jobs that never seemed to lead anywhere. She accepted those aspects of her life as events to be expected, but she finally sought therapy when yet another relationship ended badly. She wanted to learn why she was so unlucky.

Over a period of several months, her therapist was able to help her understand that her view of the world contributed to her failures. With much encouragement from her therapist, she was able to think about her long-term goals and what she would need to do to accomplish them. She came to appreciate that her failed relationships had more to do with her making foolish decisions than bad luck. Nina experienced several setbacks along the way, but over the following two years she was able to make enough adjustments to her locus of control that she could see her life moving in a positive direction.

While hundreds of research studies have documented the advantages of having an internal locus of control, Rotter did argue that extremes at either end of the continuum could be harmful. While people with an extremely external locus of control may feel powerless, those with an extremely internal locus of control may not understand that sometimes there are things that we really cannot control. Dan's experience provides a clear example of this. It was his dream to be a professional golfer, and he was quite talented. He won his state high school championship and was an All-American in college. But he always fell just short of making it to the highest level of professional golf. He would tell himself that he needed to work harder, to practice more; but with each setback, he became increasingly anxious and depressed, as those with an internal locus of control are prone to do when they experience failure. Other people who aspire to success in fields in which only a few stand out—such as music, writing, and acting—

have also learned that hard work and persistence do not always pay off. The truth is that there are times when the right breaks can make all the difference. Yes, we are more likely to achieve success and happiness if we accept the premise that our efforts matter, but we have to have the wisdom, as the Serenity Prayer suggests, to know the difference.

+ 14 +

how often do you feel really good?

The following phrases describe people's feelings. Indicate the extent to which you agree that the statement describes you.

1. I often feel joy.

1	2	3	4	5
strongly disagree	disagree	neither agree nor disagree	agree	strongly agree

2. I often feel cheerful.

1	2	3	4	5
strongly disagree	disagree	neither agree nor disagree	agree	strongly agree

3. I often feel enthusiastic.

1	2	3	4	5
strongly disagree	disagree	neither agree nor disagree	agree	strongly agree

4. I often feel light-hearted.

1	2	3	4	5
strongly disagree	disagree	neither agree nor disagree	agree	strongly agree

5. I often feel lively.

1	2	3	4	5
strongly disagree	disagree	neither agree nor disagree	agree	strongly agree

6. I often feel delight.

1	2	3	4	5
strongly disagree	disagree	neither agree nor disagree	agree	strongly agree

7. I often feel happy.

1	2	3	4	5
strongly disagree	disagree	neither agree nor disagree	agree	strongly agree

8. I often feel contented.

1	2	3	4	5
strongly disagree	disagree	neither agree nor disagree	agree	strongly agree

9. I often feel alert.

1	2	3	4	5
strongly disagree	disagree	neither agree nor disagree	agree	strongly agree

10. I often feel confident.

1	2	3	4	5
strongly disagree	disagree	neither agree nor disagree	agree	strongly agree

11. I often feel eager.

1	2	3	4	5
strongly disagree	disagree	neither agree nor disagree	agree	strongly agree

12. I often feel strong.

1	2	3	4	5
strongly disagree	disagree	neither agree nor disagree	agree	strongly agree

13. I often feel interested.

1	2	3	4	5
strongly disagree	disagree	neither agree nor disagree	agree	strongly agree

14. I often feel determined.

1	2	3	4	5
strongly disagree	disagree	neither agree nor disagree	agree	strongly agree

15. I often feel focused.

1	2	3	4	5
strongly disagree	disagree	neither agree nor disagree	agree	strongly agree

16. I often feel energetic.

1	2	3	4	5
strongly disagree	disagree	neither agree nor disagree	agree	strongly agree

+ scoring

Add your points together for your total score on the Positive Mood Test. High scores indicate a high level of experiencing positive mood states.

POSITIVE MOOD SCORE	PERCENTILE
55	**85**
50	70
45	**50**
40	30
35	**15**

+ about the positive mood test

Psychologists have been studying negative emotions such as anxiety, guilt, and sadness for more than a century, but it has only been over the past decade or so that they have begun to pay serious attention to positive emotions, also called positive mood states. The eminent psychologist Paul Meehl was one of the first to argue that people may differ in their "hedonic capacity." He argued that some people were genetically programmed to be happier than others and that this difference in "cerebral joy-juice" might have important implications in clinical practice. For most of the past century, a key assumption has been that the way to help people feel better was to reduce, if not eliminate, their negative emotions. That is, if therapists could reduce guilt, people would feel joyful; if therapists could eliminate sadness, people would feel happy. Meehl proposed, however, that positive mood states were independent from negative mood states, and recent research largely supports his assertion. This is an extremely important finding because it suggests that happiness will not necessarily surface once sadness is eliminated, nor will joy appear once guilt is vanquished.

The current consensus among experts is that positive and negative mood states are two relatively independent dimensions of emotional experience, and they both developed over human history to serve different evolutionary tasks. We experience negative emotions primarily to keep us out of trouble. They motivate us to avoid doing things that will lead to harm, punishment, or pain. Positive mood states, on the other hand, motivate us to seek out resources such as warmth, food, drink, and even sexual partners, that ensure the survival of the species. In our current state of civilization, mood states no longer play as important a role in our survival as they once did; they have become a quality-of-life issue. We all would like to earn a high score on the Positive Mood Test simply because it feels good to experience these emotions.

Research over the past ten years has taught us several interesting things about positive mood states. First, we know that mood states fluctuate more for young people than for older adults. Psychologist David Watson and his colleagues have found that moods begin to stabilize around age thirty. Second, our mood states tend to be consistent regardless of what we are doing at any particular moment. People who are typically in a good mood at work also tend to be in a good mood when they are socializing. People who tend to be in a bad mood when alone are likely to be in a bad mood when they are with others. Happy, cheerful people tend to be happy and cheerful regardless of what they are doing or who they are with.

Watson's research has also addressed the question of why some people experience more positive moods than others, and, as is the case with so many human characteristics, our genetic heritage plays an important role. But as important as our genes may be, life experiences play an even larger role in influencing how often we experience positive mood states. Perhaps the most important of these life experiences is socializing. People who frequently experience positive moods spend more time with good friends and relatives, they make more new acquaintances, and they are involved in more social organizations. Watson recognizes that people who are often in a good mood are more likely to do these kinds of things, but he also reports evidence that doing these things serves to increase the frequency of positive moods. It is important to note that Watson found that it is not necessary to be young, beautiful, or rich to be happy. He reported that it is possible for virtually anyone, regardless of his or her life circumstances, to experience substantial levels of positive emotions.

If you had a low score on the Positive Moods Test, there are steps you can take to feel happier more often. Although research on positive moods is so recent that therapies to address this issue have yet to be proven effective, there are certain principles that appear to be important. First, the road to a better mood is through action rather than thought. While changing one's thoughts (an approach called cognitive behavior therapy) is quite effective in eliminating negative moods such as anxiety or depression, it does not work as well in increasing positive moods. Watson has recommended two courses of action: increased socializing and increased physical activity. And these two goals often go hand in hand. As I mention in Chapter 16, I was able to increase my positive moods by playing golf more often. I believe the mere act of walking about five miles several days per week had a significant effect; but golf is a social activity, so I spent more time talking with friends. Other people have had the same experience that I did after joining an aerobics class or playing pick-up basketball games during their lunch hour. The important point is that you cannot wait to feel good before getting back out into the world; you have to get out there and the good feelings will follow.

A second observation offered by Watson is that the process of striving toward goals is more crucial to feelings of happiness than the actual accomplishment of those goals. We have to be involved, we have to stretch our minds or our bodies in an attempt to accomplish something difficult if we are to experience positive moods. We have all heard stories about people who said the happiest times of their lives were when they were struggling to make it through graduate school or to get the business off the ground. So many of us have the painful experience of discovering that when we finally reach our goals we feel empty, even miserable. The solution, of course, is to continually set new goals, even if they may appear to be modest.

I know one man who loved his job as CEO of a medium-size company and was looking forward to his retirement, when he could relax and enjoy the fruits of his hard work, only to discover that most of his days were lonely and empty. He rediscovered his capacity for positive moods when he became interested in designing Web sites. Initially, he wanted only a home page to make it easy for his family to see the photos he and his wife took on their retirement travels. But he attacked his hobby the same way he had attacked his job, and in no time he was designing sites for his friends and a few small businesses. If we do not have something to look forward to when we get out of bed in the morning, it should come as no surprise that we will not experience many positive mood states.

A third, very simple recommendation (although often difficult to implement) by Watson is to make sure you get enough sleep. It has been well documented that many people in our society are sleep deprived, and it is difficult, if not impossible, to feel energetic and alert when we are tired. A corollary of this recommendation is to be attentive to our biological rhythms and cycles. We all have cycles when we will feel energetic and alert at some points during the day and tired and lethargic at others. Watson recommends that we become thoroughly familiar with our particular cycle and to tackle difficult, complex tasks when we are especially alert and energetic. Too many of us try to mask our lethargic periods with an extra cup of coffee or two, and it doesn't work very well. If we expect too much of ourselves during the low periods, it will likely leave us feeling frustrated and angry.

health

+ + +

are you protecting your health?

The following phrases describe people's behaviors, attitudes, and feelings. Indicate the extent to which you agree that the statement describes you.

1. I am in good health.

1	2	3	4	5
strongly disagree	disagree	neither agree nor disagree	agree	strongly agree

2. I have more health problems than most people.

1	2	3	4	5
strongly disagree	disagree	neither agree nor disagree	agree	strongly agree

3. I visit the doctor more often than most people.

1	2	3	4	5
strongly disagree	disagree	neither agree nor disagree	agree	strongly agree

4. I am being treated for several serious illnesses.

1	2	3	4	5
strongly disagree	disagree	neither agree nor disagree	agree	strongly agree

5. I smoke.

1	2	3	4	5
strongly disagree	disagree	neither agree nor disagree	agree	strongly agree

6. I have several drinks per day.

1	2	3	4	5
strongly disagree	disagree	neither agree nor disagree	agree	strongly agree

7. I eat more red meat than most people.

1	2	3	4	5
strongly disagree	disagree	neither agree nor disagree	agree	strongly agree

8. I eat more fruit and vegetables than most people.

1	2	3	4	5
strongly disagree	disagree	neither agree nor disagree	agree	strongly agree

9. I am overweight.

1	2	3	4	5
strongly disagree	disagree	neither agree nor disagree	agree	strongly agree

10. I walk thirty minutes per day, five or six times per week.

1	2	3	4	5
strongly disagree	disagree	neither agree nor disagree	agree	strongly agree

11. I regularly do exercises to increase my flexibility.

1	2	3	4	5
strongly disagree	disagree	neither agree nor disagree	agree	strongly agree

12. I regularly do exercises to increase my strength.

1	2	3	4	5
strongly disagree	disagree	neither agree nor disagree	agree	strongly agree

13. I regularly do exercises that increase my heart rate.

1	2	3	4	5
strongly disagree	disagree	neither agree nor disagree	agree	strongly agree

14. I have regular medical examinations.

1	2	3	4	5
strongly disagree	disagree	neither agree nor disagree	agree	strongly agree

15. I have a medical problem that limits my independence.

1	2	3	4	5
strongly disagree	disagree	neither agree nor disagree	agree	strongly agree

16. I have a medical problem that limits my mobility.

1	2	3	4	5
strongly disagree	disagree	neither agree nor disagree	agree	strongly agree

+ scoring

The first step is to reverse score items 2, 3, 4, 5, 6, 7, 9, 15, and 16. For these items, if you circled 5, change it to a 1, a 4 becomes a 2, a 3 remains a 3, a 2 becomes a 4, and a 1 becomes a 5. After you have made these changes, add your points together for your total score on the Health Test. High scores indicate a high degree of good health habits.

HEALTH SCORE	PERCENTILE
63	**85**
59	70
54	**50**
49	30
45	**15**

+ about the health test

If you don't have your health nothing else matters, right? Well, not exactly. It turns out that being in good health is not very important to our happiness. There is a slight—very slight—relationship between good health and happiness, but there is strong evidence that good health matters less to our happiness than most of us might think. One study, for instance, found that

58 percent of men who survived a first heart attack reported enjoying their lives more than they had before their illness. Furthermore, these men believed that they had benefited from their experience. They reported making positive changes in their values, philosophy of life, and health habits. Even those people who experience a catastrophic accident that leaves them without the use of their legs show only a slight decline in their happiness. Seven weeks after their accident they report more positive emotions than negative, and after two years they are only slightly less happy than their nonparalyzed peers.

It does appear, however, that the health-happiness link is stronger for the elderly, although it is not completely clear why this is so. Also, there is evidence that people with several illnesses are less happy than those with a single malady, so perhaps the link is stronger for the elderly because they are more likely to have multiple problems. A second possible explanation is that when the elderly have serious medical problems they are more likely to experience changes in their living situation and to suffer a loss of social support. When a forty-year-old, for example, suffers from a serious illness, he or she is more likely to be able to recuperate at home with family support and encouragement. A seventy-five-year-old may have to be moved to a nursing home because the spouse is either deceased or physically unable to provide the necessary care. Whatever the reason for the health-happiness link among the elderly, it should remind us that it is never too early for us to begin to do everything we can to preserve and enhance our health. Having a healthy lifestyle may not mean much to our happiness when we are young or even middle-aged, but it will increase our odds of living long enough to be included among the elderly one day and will enhance our enjoyment of life once we get there.

Even among the elderly ill there is wide variation in happiness levels. I saw these differences firsthand when I worked in a nursing home that provided long-term care for the elderly. All of the residents were seriously ill and unable to care for themselves, and it is true that many of them were quite miserable and depressed. They rarely left their rooms, rarely spoke to anyone, and spent most of their waking hours numbly watching the television screen, never bothering to change the channel. There were others, however, who appeared to be happy and cheerful despite their severe limitations. Verona, for example, had a stroke that resulted in her having little control of the left side of her body, but she spent much of her time riding her motorized chair up and down the hallways chatting with the other residents and offering encouragement to those who needed it. She was especially happy on Tuesdays, the day she had her hair done. She wanted to look nice when her children and grandchildren visited her. Vincent lost both of his legs as a consequence of diabetes, but on sunny days he was a constant fixture on the front porch. Yes, he liked to be out there so he could smoke, but he had also made friends with several people who lived in the neighborhood. His conversations with them were punctuated with frequent laughter.

The first three items on the Health Test are important because it has been found that there is a stronger link between happiness and perceived health than with actual health. People who worry about their health are less happy than nonworriers, even though their actual health may be better. The link between happiness and perceived health seems to be explained by the observation that health worriers tend to receive high scores on measures of neurosis. And neurotic people are unhappy people.

In this day and age when we are bombarded with information about health, it is obvious to all that many of the items on the Health Test reflect habits that preserve and enhance our health. As I mentioned earlier, our health may not matter much to our happiness now, but it is likely to make a difference as we get older. And just in case you do not fully appreciate how important our habits are to our health, consider this: A century ago, infectious diseases dominated the top ten leading causes of death, but today, now that we have effective medications and vaccinations, this list is primarily made up of diseases that reflect lifestyle choices. Fully 50 percent of deaths can be attributed to bad health habits. So now is the time to begin to eat right and exercise regularly, and to give up those vices. Stop smoking, limit your alcohol intake to a single drink per day, and lose those extra pounds. As I know all too well, these changes can be very difficult to implement. I love ice cream and thick, juicy steaks, and to me, vegetables are at best a tasteless obligation. But diabetes runs in my family so I am struggling to lose thirty pounds (I've got ten more to go). Like me, you do not have to be perfect in your efforts to change but you must be persistent. I've lost my twenty pounds over a period of three years by making more good choices than bad, although I continue to make a number of the latter. I simply cannot resist a two-for-one sale on ice cream. So, like me, when you make a bad choice, do not view it as a reason to abandon your attempts to change. View it as a bump on the road to eventual success. As long as you keep trying, you have the ability to change your life.

One final thought. Remember the men who enjoyed their lives more after they had a heart attack? Well, eight years after their illness, the 58 percent of the heart attack sufferers who found benefits in their experience were in better health and were less likely to have experienced a second heart attack than the 42 percent of them who were unable to find anything positive about their illness. Part of the explanation for this is that the men with positive attitudes were more likely to make the changes they needed to protect their health, but there is more to it than this.

Over the past decade, evidence has begun to reveal that our thoughts and feelings—our attitudes—can have a direct influence on our body's physiological mechanisms. Much of this research has focused on the effects of stress, and it is clear that negative emotions can impair our immune system's ability to function, making us vulnerable to a variety of diseases. While we now know that people with a positive attitude, that is, happy people, are less likely to become ill, researchers are currently exploring the possibility that happiness may actually enhance our body's ability to fight off disease. Regardless of the outcome of this research, it is clear that it is possible for both negative and positive cycles to develop. Unhappy people have impaired immune system functioning, which leads to more health problems. And this, in turn, leads to more unhappiness, especially among the elderly. So now is the time for us to begin creating a positive cycle for ourselves. Let us develop good health habits that will lead to greater happiness as we get older, which will stabilize and possibly enhance our body's ability to resist disease.

+ 16 +

are you engaged with the world around you?

The following phrases describe people's behaviors, attitudes, and feelings. Indicate the extent to which you agree that the statement describes you.

1. I enjoy discussing movies and books with friends.

1	2	3	4	5
strongly disagree	disagree	neither agree nor disagree	agree	strongly agree

2. I find discussions about world affairs interesting.

1	2	3	4	5
strongly disagree	disagree	neither agree nor disagree	agree	strongly agree

3. I try to avoid complex people.

1	2	3	4	5
strongly disagree	disagree	neither agree nor disagree	agree	strongly agree

4. I prefer to stick with things I know.

1	2	3	4	5
strongly disagree	disagree	neither agree nor disagree	agree	strongly agree

5. I have little patience for philosophical discussions.

1	2	3	4	5
strongly disagree	disagree	neither agree nor disagree	agree	strongly agree

6. I love to learn new things.

1	2	3	4	5
strongly disagree	disagree	neither agree nor disagree	agree	strongly agree

7. I try to examine myself objectively.

1	2	3	4	5
strongly disagree	disagree	neither agree nor disagree	agree	strongly agree

8. I have a wide variety of interests.

1	2	3	4	5
strongly disagree	disagree	neither agree nor disagree	agree	strongly agree

9. I want to increase my knowledge.

1	2	3	4	5
strongly disagree	disagree	neither agree nor disagree	agree	strongly agree

10. I can become lost in a book.

1	2	3	4	5
strongly disagree	disagree	neither agree nor disagree	agree	strongly agree

11. I have no interest in art.

1	2	3	4	5
strongly disagree	disagree	neither agree nor disagree	agree	strongly agree

12. I enjoy talking about national politics.

1	2	3	4	5
strongly disagree	disagree	neither agree nor disagree	agree	strongly agree

13. Learning more about other cultures interests me.

1	2	3	4	5
strongly disagree	disagree	neither agree nor disagree	agree	strongly agree

14. I avoid reading anything too heavy.

1	2	3	4	5
strongly disagree	disagree	neither agree nor disagree	agree	strongly agree

15. I do not enjoy classical music.

1	2	3	4	5
strongly disagree	disagree	neither agree nor disagree	agree	strongly agree

+ scoring

The first step is to reverse score items 3, 4, 5, 11, 14, and 15. For these items, if you circled 5, change it to a 1, a 4 becomes a 2, a 3 remains a 3, a 2 becomes a 4, and a 1 becomes a 5. After you have made these changes, add your points together for your total score on the Intellectual Openness Test. High scores indicate a high degree of intellectual openness.

INTELLECTUAL OPENNESS SCORE	PERCENTILE
54	85
49	70
44	50
39	30
34	15

+ about the intellectual openness test

There is a tried-and-true prescription for unhappiness. Get yourself out of bed every morning and go to work at a job in which you take little pride or joy. Then come home every evening, fix yourself something quick and easy to eat, and plop down in your favorite chair to watch reruns on cable. To make this approach work, it is important that you take no interest in the news, your neighbors, or even your friends. Do not read anything or try anything new. And if anyone tries to talk with you about what is going on in the world, let your eyes glaze over and get back to your favorite chair as quickly as possible. How do I know this will work? Because I tried it for nearly a year after my divorce, and it worked beautifully. I was extremely unhappy. If you received a low score on the Intellectual Openness Test, I'm willing to bet that you have firsthand knowledge of just how effective a strategy like this can be.

It was obvious to me during the year that I spent perfecting this strategy (I don't believe there is an episode of *Law & Order* I haven't seen at least three times) that a very low level of intellectual openness can be a sign of depression. But, as I discovered, the link between depression and intellectual stultification may not be straightforward. I tried taking antidepressant medication, and while it took the edge off my misery, it was not enough to entice me to give up my *Law & Order* reruns. I finally decided that the time had come for me to do something proactive about my situation, so I gave up the medication and vowed to reengage myself with the rest of the world. A colleague of mine has called this the GOYA technique—get off your ass.

I began slowly. Despite feeling as if I were lacking the energy, I forced myself to play golf with my friends and spend a little time with them at the nineteenth hole. I cut back on the *Law & Order* reruns to read the books that for so many years I couldn't find the time for. And the most drastic step of all: I dedicated two evenings each week to spending time with old friends and getting to know new ones.

It was a struggle. There were many mornings when I was leaving for the golf course and many evenings when, on the way to meet a new friend, that I chastised myself for making the commitment. I wanted to stay home close to my favorite chair. But I forced myself to go, and by the time I got home I couldn't deny that I almost always felt better. It took several months, but the time did come when I could feel a flash of joy as I looked out at the early-morning dew on the golf course.

As part of my regimen to expand my horizons, I gave up *Law & Order* to watch the History and Discovery channels. One evening I saw a program about the changes that had taken place in China since the late 1990s. It was a country that had interested me since I was in college, and given my new single status, I realized there was no reason not to act on this interest. I searched the Internet, found a great price for a tour and planned to see the Three Gorges over my spring break. On the flight from Guangzhou to Chongqing, I was seated next to an attractive Chinese woman who asked if she could use me to practice her English. I readily agreed, and by the time we landed, we had made arrangements to meet for dinner. Now, after nine months and three more trips to China, we are engaged and will be married by the time this book is published.

I was lucky, very lucky. But I would never have met this wonderful woman had I not made the effort to increase my intellectual openness and reengage myself with the world. Even had we not met, I am certain that I would be much happier as my attempts to become involved with the world around me took root. Tina simply speeded up the process.

Many of you also may have lost your intellectual openness as a result of depression, but that is not the only route to couch-potato status. Richard, for instance, had the usual range of interests through college. He had lots of friends, and he loved sharing his philosophy of life with them late into the night over a few beers (or perhaps something more aromatic). Upon graduation, he accepted a job twelve hundred miles away in a city where he knew no one. All of his colleagues were at least a few years older, married, and more settled than he. So other than sporadic invitations to dinner, Richard spent most of his evenings alone. He tried a few bars that catered to people his age, but he felt uncomfortable going by himself. Six months later Richard purchased a satellite dish, comforting himself with the thought that it takes a while to get to know people in a new town.

Richard had never developed the habit of intellectual openness, and while it is difficult to say whether it was his inertia or his anxiety that was holding him back, it did take a gentle push from a counselor to get him started. His painful loneliness motivated him to be a faster study than I was, and he embraced his counselor's advice to pursue his interests to meet people with whom he had something in common. Richard was not sure where to start, but a newspaper article about a local state senate race caught his eye one morning, and so he decided to attend a debate between the candidates. The debate touched on social issues that he had spent countless hours discussing with his friends during college, and Richard was hooked. He began to read everything he could about his state's economic problems, to do volunteer work for a couple of local organizations, and within a year discovered that he didn't have enough time to do everything that needed doing. He made a number of friends along the way, which was important to Richard, but not more important than the excitement he felt about the new experiences he was having.

The items on the Intellectual Openness Test can be a little misleading. It is easy to get the impression that one has to be an introspective egghead who is interested in art, politics, different cultures, and the like to have enough intellectual openness to be happy. I don't think that is necessarily true. It is not essential to have any specific interest; however, it is crucial to have an interest in something. I believe it is human nature to be curious, to want to know more about the world around us. We do not need to make grand discoveries to be happy, but we must continue to learn. It can be something as simple as learning to play a new tune on a harmonica or discovering that a particular herb adds a satisfying dimension to our favorite dish. We must strive to expand our world, or surely it will contract until it suffocates us.

+ 17 +

how emotionally stable are you?

The following phrases describe people's behaviors, attitudes, and feelings. Indicate the extent to which you agree that the statement describes you.

1. I am relaxed most of the time.

1 strongly disagree	2 disagree	3 neither agree nor disagree	4 agree	5 strongly agree

2. I tend to worry about things.

1 strongly disagree	2 disagree	3 neither agree nor disagree	4 agree	5 strongly agree

3. I am easily disturbed.

1 strongly disagree	2 disagree	3 neither agree nor disagree	4 agree	5 strongly agree

4. I seldom feel blue.

1	2	3	4	5
strongly disagree	disagree	neither agree nor disagree	agree	strongly agree

5. I get upset easily.

1	2	3	4	5
strongly disagree	disagree	neither agree nor disagree	agree	strongly agree

6. I change my mood a lot.

1	2	3	4	5
strongly disagree	disagree	neither agree nor disagree	agree	strongly agree

7. I have frequent mood swings.

1	2	3	4	5
strongly disagree	disagree	neither agree nor disagree	agree	strongly agree

8. I get irritated easily.

1	2	3	4	5
strongly disagree	disagree	neither agree nor disagree	agree	strongly agree

9. I often feel blue.

1	2	3	4	5
strongly disagree	disagree	neither agree nor disagree	agree	strongly agree

10. I am not easily bothered by things.

1	2	3	4	5
strongly disagree	disagree	neither agree nor disagree	agree	strongly agree

11. I rarely get irritated.

1	2	3	4	5
strongly disagree	disagree	neither agree nor disagree	agree	strongly agree

12. I get angry easily.

1	2	3	4	5
strongly disagree	disagree	neither agree nor disagree	agree	strongly agree

13. I panic easily.

1	2	3	4	5
strongly disagree	disagree	neither agree nor disagree	agree	strongly agree

14. I feel threatened easily.

1	2	3	4	5
strongly disagree	disagree	neither agree nor disagree	agree	strongly agree

15. I seldom get mad.

1	2	3	4	5
strongly disagree	disagree	neither agree nor disagree	agree	strongly agree

16. I become overwhelmed by emotions.

1	2	3	4	5
strongly disagree	disagree	neither agree nor disagree	agree	strongly agree

17. I take offense easily.

1	2	3	4	5
strongly disagree	disagree	neither agree nor disagree	agree	strongly agree

18. I get caught up in my problems.

1	2	3	4	5
strongly disagree	disagree	neither agree nor disagree	agree	strongly agree

19. I grumble about things.

1	2	3	4	5
strongly disagree	disagree	neither agree nor disagree	agree	strongly agree

20. I get stressed out easily.

1	2	3	4	5
strongly disagree	disagree	neither agree nor disagree	agree	strongly agree

+ scoring

The first step is to reverse score items 2, 3, 5, 6, 7, 8, 9, 12, 13, 14, 16, 17, 18, 19, and 20. For these items, if you circled 5, change it to a 1, a 4 becomes a 2, a 3 remains a 3, a 2 becomes a 4, and a 1 becomes a 5. After you have made these changes, add your points together for your total score on the Emotional Stability Test. High scores indicate a high degree of emotional stability.

EMOTIONAL STABILITY SCORE	PERCENTILE
82	85
77	70
71	50
65	30
60	15

+ about the emotional stability test

Emotional stability is at the opposite end of the continuum of a trait you may be more familiar with: neuroticism. As the items on the Emotional Stability Test suggest, neurotic people are those who become upset easily; frequently experience intense, negative emotions; and generally believe life is more difficult for them than it is for others. Emotionally stable people, on the other hand, are generally calm and slow to anger; while they are certainly capable of experiencing negative emotions, such feelings occur less frequently than they do in their less stable peers. In recent years, several studies have found that emotional stability is the most important personality characteristic in terms of its contribution to happiness. So if you received a score below the 30th percentile on the Emotional Stability Test, it is probable that you will be happier if you address this critical issue.

Emotional stability is especially important because it has been found to be related to one's happiness over long periods of time.

Researchers Paul Costa and Robert McCrae, who constructed one of the most widely used tests of personality called the NEO Personality Inventory, found that a measure of emotional stability was able to predict one's level of happiness ten years later. People with low scores on this test cannot afford to simply wait for things to get better because they probably won't. They must take action if they want to feel more satisfied with their lives.

If you did receive a low score on this test, the odds are good that you do feel unhappy much of the time and that it is difficult for you to cope with the day-to-day challenges of life. You may want to consult a professional to help you implement the changes needed to turn things around, but it is possible to do it on your own with the help of a good self-help guide. One of my favorites is Albert Ellis's *A Guide to Rational Living*, first published in 1961 with a third edition published in 1998. That it continues to sell well forty years after it was first published attests to the soundness of Ellis's advice. I cannot do justice to his approach in just a few pages, but let me introduce his central idea.

Ellis argued that while most of us blame either others or certain events for making us feel upset or unhappy, it is our own thoughts that are the source of our misery. To illustrate, let's suppose that our friend Joe tells us that he is depressed because his girlfriend has announced that she never wants to see him again. Joe blames his former partner for his distress because had she stayed with him, he insists, he would be okay. But according to Ellis, it is not the event of being dumped that has caused Joe to be unhappy, it is what he is saying to himself about being dumped that is making him miserable. He is probably having thoughts such as, "I'll never again find anyone who loves me," or "I'm destined to be lonely for the rest of my life," or "She was the perfect woman for me and I'll never find someone like her again." Ellis insists that such thoughts are neither logical nor rational. And it is because Joe is saying such illogical and irrational things to himself that he is depressed.

It follows, then, that the key to Joe's feeling better is for him to eliminate his irrational and illogical thoughts and to replace them with logical and rational self-statements. It would be rational, for example, for him to think, "It's too bad that she left me, but there are lots of other available women in the world," or "I've been between relationships before, and I know that sooner or later I'll meet someone new," or "She did have many special qualities, but most women have their own special qualities." Understandably, if Joe says these kinds of things to himself, he will feel much better than if he tells himself all of the previous negative irrational statements.

The basic principles of Ellis's approach are relatively simple and straightforward, but it does take effort and persistence to implement his ideas. The kinds of thoughts we have in reaction to the world around us are the result of a lifetime of training; they are not easily discarded for a new perspective. Indeed, it may be difficult for us to even appreciate the irrationality of many of our thoughts because they are so much a part of us.

Jan, for instance, was almost constantly in a state of turmoil because her husband and children did not adhere to her rigid standards of tidiness and cleanliness. When I suggested that it was not her family's behavior but rather what she was telling herself about their behavior that was upsetting her, she became angry. She insisted that she was not saying anything to herself about the disorderly state of her house (which to her could mean that a cushion was out of place) but that she only wanted things to look nice so she could feel comfortable. But after lengthy discussion, Jan did acknowledge that she held certain beliefs about what a clean and orderly house meant to her. It meant that she was a good wife and mother. And when her family failed to maintain her standards, it meant that they did not love and appreciate her. It took several months of practice before she could begin to feel comfortable when faced with a mess, making statements such as "When you have a family, these things will always happen" and "I'm lucky to have a family I love so much." Jan never became a relaxed housekeeper, but she was able to change enough so she could accept some disorder with equanimity.

I would guess that many of you who scored low on the Emotional Stability Test have the same problem that Jan did—your irrational thoughts have become so automatic that it is difficult for you to identify them. If you agreed with item 20, for example, "I get stressed out easily," you may not know what you are thinking when you feel stressed out, only that certain events result in your having those feelings. For this approach to work for you, you will need to accept the premise that when you identify your irrational thoughts and substitute more rational and logical ones, you will feel better. So, even if it is difficult for you to identify your specific irrational thoughts, try to imagine what you could say to yourself that would be more logical and rational.

Suppose you feel stressed out because you have to stop by the grocery store on the way home from work before preparing dinner for your family. You could remind yourself that "it's not the end of the world if we eat dinner a half hour later than usual" or "I'm lucky to have a family to take care of." After practicing these more logical self-statements, the irrational thoughts you were having may well become clearer to you.

Changing the pattern of thoughts you have developed over a lifetime is an arduous task and one that you might need help with, but if you received a low score on this scale, it is critical for you to do so. I believe that emotional stability is the cornerstone of happiness. All of the topics discussed in this book were included because they are related to our potential for happiness, though it is possible to be happy even if we are deficient in many of them. People can be happy, for instance, even though they never have sex or never have a romantic relationship. But I do not think it is possible to achieve more than momentary episodes of happiness without emotional stability. Recall Costa and McCrae's finding that people low in emotional stability were still unhappy ten years later. I urge those of you who received low scores on this test to make the effort to change. If you find it difficult to do so on your own, do not hesitate to consult a professional. It is that important.

are you a spiritual person?

The following phrases describe people's beliefs, attitudes, and feelings. Indicate the extent to which you agree that the statement describes you.

1. I believe it is important for people to find meaning in their lives.

1	2	3	4	5
strongly disagree	disagree	neither agree nor disagree	agree	strongly agree

2. I believe there are forces in the universe that will never be explained by science.

1	2	3	4	5
strongly disagree	disagree	neither agree nor disagree	agree	strongly agree

3. I believe in a creator.

1	2	3	4	5
strongly disagree	disagree	neither agree nor disagree	agree	strongly agree

4. I believe things happen for a reason.

1	2	3	4	5
strongly disagree	disagree	neither agree nor disagree	agree	strongly agree

5. I believe human life is nothing more than an accident of evolution.

1	2	3	4	5
strongly disagree	disagree	neither agree nor disagree	agree	strongly agree

6. The human spirit can transcend death.

1	2	3	4	5
strongly disagree	disagree	neither agree nor disagree	agree	strongly agree

7. People are more than their biology.

1	2	3	4	5
strongly disagree	disagree	neither agree nor disagree	agree	strongly agree

8. Human behavior is the product of nature and nurture.

1	2	3	4	5
strongly disagree	disagree	neither agree nor disagree	agree	strongly agree

9. I have experienced moments of oneness with the universe.

1	2	3	4	5
strongly disagree	disagree	neither agree nor disagree	agree	strongly agree

10. I would have to be successful in order to be happy.

1	2	3	4	5
strongly disagree	disagree	neither agree nor disagree	agree	strongly agree

11. The universe is not merely an accident of nature.

1	2	3	4	5
strongly disagree	disagree	neither agree nor disagree	agree	strongly agree

12. I find the pursuit of material possessions as a means of securing happiness distasteful.

1	2	3	4	5
strongly disagree	disagree	neither agree nor disagree	agree	strongly agree

13. There is a balance and order to nature.

1	2	3	4	5
strongly disagree	disagree	neither agree nor disagree	agree	strongly agree

14. Ceremonial occasions reflect the richness of human existence.

1	2	3	4	5
strongly disagree	disagree	neither agree nor disagree	agree	strongly agree

15. I often feel highly emotional during certain ceremonial occasions.

1	2	3	4	5
strongly disagree	disagree	neither agree nor disagree	agree	strongly agree

16. Too many people today continue to believe superstitions that originated in primitive times.

1	2	3	4	5
strongly disagree	disagree	neither agree nor disagree	agree	strongly agree

+ scoring

The first step is to reverse score items 5, 8, 10, 11, and 16. For these items, if you circled 5, change it to a 1, a 4 becomes a 2, a 3 remains a 3, a 2 becomes a 4, and a 1 becomes a 5. After you have made these changes, add your points together for your total score on the Spirituality Test. High scores indicate a high degree of spirituality.

SPIRITUALITY SCORE	PERCENTILE
63	85
58	70
52	50
46	30
41	15

+ about the spirituality test

Spirituality and research psychology got off to a rocky start.
More than forty years ago psychologists began to investigate the
characteristics of religious people and, for the most part, the results of these studies were not flattering. Perhaps the most salient
finding was that people who considered themselves highly religious were more likely to be bigots and were generally more intol-
erant than their nonreligious counterparts. Research in this area
languished for several decades, but with the advent of positive
psychology in the 1990s, there has been a renewed interest in these
topics and a very different picture of the implications of spiritual
beliefs began to emerge. Now, it would seem, there are numerous
and important benefits associated with spirituality and religiosity.

Let me pause here to define terms. When psychologists began
this line of research nearly a half century ago, they did not dis-
tinguish religiosity from spirituality. But over the past decade
theorists have not only made this distinction, they have also dis-
tinguished among several forms of spirituality and among several
forms of religiosity. Perhaps because this line of work is so new,
a consensus regarding definitions of these terms has yet to
be reached, but there is general agreement that while spirituality
and religiosity overlap they are distinct orientations. Religion
usually involves a more formal set of beliefs that are often insti-
tutionalized, whereas spirituality is more personal and subjective.
Religious people may be spiritual, but not all are. And while many
spiritual people are religious, there are many exceptions as well.
Some theorists have argued that the concept of God is a crucial
component of spirituality, but others maintain that spirituality
does not demand a belief in the divine or the supernatural.

I constructed the Spirituality Test to reflect the latter position,
using a definition offered by Bowling Green State University psy-

chologists Kenneth Pargament and Annette Mahoney. They wrote, "Spirituality is a process that speaks to the greatest of our potentials." Spiritual people believe that we are more than mere flesh and blood; they believe that there is meaning to be found in our existence, that we are not simply passing time until we die, that our time on this earth is valuable, and that we should make the most of it in a way that elevates the human condition. And, as I have already hinted, recent research has found that there are a number of benefits associated with such a view of life and of the world in which we live.

Because this work is so recent, many researchers have combined religiosity and spirituality when investigating the influence of these beliefs. It will probably be several years before we have information about the unique benefits of spirituality and religiosity, so I will use the terms as if they were interchangable. But this view will probably change in the coming years.

Perhaps the most startling finding is that religious/spiritual people live longer. They are less likely to suffer from heart disease, high cholesterol, hypertension, and cancer. Also, it has been found that spiritual people have a better recovery from serious medical problems, including orthopedic impairments, alcoholism, and HIV, to name a few. Furthermore, spiritual people who suffer from serious medical problems are more likely to report higher levels of satisfaction with their lives than their nonspiritual counterparts. Spirituality and religiosity have also been found to be related to mental health. People with this perspective on life are less likely to be depressed or lonely and, again, are more likely to be satisfied with their lives.

While the benefits of spirituality/religiosity are clear, there can be a downside, depending on the specific nature of one's spirituality. If one believes that a beneficent higher power is influencing one's fate, it can be difficult to understand why bad things happen.

In their study of the spirituality of men and women undergoing inpatient rehabilitation, psychologist Jo Kim and his colleagues found that almost one-third of these patients experienced a decline in both their spirituality and their emotional well-being during the course of their stay in the hospital. These people were likely to view themselves as victims of a cruel and capricious deity. They wondered why God was punishing them and why He hadn't protected them from this terrible illness. Most people in our society would agree that another example of the potentially harmful effects of a certain type of spirituality can be found in people who, on religious grounds, refuse medical treatment for their children. While these parents might feel comfortable with their decision, most of us would argue that in this case their spirituality is misguided.

When I think of what is good about spirituality, I cannot help but think of my mother, who is both a very spiritual and a very religious woman. She contracted poliomyelitis when she was twenty-five years old and spent more than a year in a hospital, much of the time lying helpless in an iron lung. She spent several more years making daily trips to the hospital for rehabilitation, and the result was that she learned to walk with the aid of a leg brace and crutches. Although she must have had moments when her spirituality and faith in God faltered, I never saw them. She never blamed God for her illness but instead thanked Him for giving her the strength to cope with it. She never experienced any bitterness about her limitations but always searched for ways to help those around her. My mother's story is a perfect example of the healing and inspiring effects of a rich spiritual life.

I have to confess that despite my firsthand knowledge of the powerful effects that spirituality can have, I received a rather low score on this scale. Perhaps it has something to do with my training as a scientist, perhaps (I hope this isn't the case) it reflects a more natural cynicism. But I am trying to change. My divorce of a few years ago taught me that hard work, financial rewards, and even a little public recognition do not mean much in the long run. It taught me that I cannot control everything about my life and that I must treasure and nurture that which is truly valuable.

Pargament talked about this most eloquently. He pointed out that much of psychology is about control. We psychologists try to help our clients control their thoughts and their behavior, and if we are Freudians, we even try to control their unconscious. But there is much about our lives that we cannot control, such as birth, death, accidents, illnesses, or the loss of a child or spouse. A sense of spirituality can help us understand and cope with these uncontrollables and, I believe, help us appreciate more fully what is good and valuable in our lives.

Perhaps because I am in the very early stages of trying to develop a sense of spirituality, I cannot fully explain the process to you. But I can tell you about some of the changes I have made in an attempt to get there. I value the little moments—a conversation with one of my sons, for instance—and I take the time to experience them. Ten years ago I chased away anyone who came into my study while I was writing. Today, I welcome the interruption. Ten years ago I took my first wife for granted. Although I was a good husband in many ways, I failed to tell her how important our relationship was to me. Now, I never let a day go by without ensuring that Tina knows how much she means to me.

I can feel the change. Despite the countless serious problems in the world, I feel good about the world. I believe we humans have made much progress over the past century, and I expect that we will make much more over the next. I hope that I can contribute to this in some small way, and I hope that by developing a sense of spirituality, you too can feel this way.

how well do you bounce back?

The following phrases describe people's behaviors, attitudes, and feelings. Indicate the extent to which you agree that the statement describes you.

1. I remain calm even when I am under a great deal of pressure.

1	2	3	4	5
strongly disagree	disagree	neither agree nor disagree	agree	strongly agree

2. If I make a mistake under stress, I can forget about it and move on.

1	2	3	4	5
strongly disagree	disagree	neither agree nor disagree	agree	strongly agree

3. I have the ability to deal effectively with difficult situations.

1 strongly disagree	2 disagree	3 neither agree nor disagree	4 agree	5 strongly agree

4. During stressful times, I feel very isolated.

1 strongly disagree	2 disagree	3 neither agree nor disagree	4 agree	5 strongly agree

5. When bad things happen to me, I try to use it as an opportunity to learn something important.

1 strongly disagree	2 disagree	3 neither agree nor disagree	4 agree	5 strongly agree

6. I feel frightened during stressful times.

1 strongly disagree	2 disagree	3 neither agree nor disagree	4 agree	5 strongly agree

7. Often something good can come out of tragedy.

1 strongly disagree	2 disagree	3 neither agree nor disagree	4 agree	5 strongly agree

8. I can find humor in stressful times.

1 strongly disagree	2 disagree	3 neither agree nor disagree	4 agree	5 strongly agree

9. There are usually several options when dealing with stressful situations.

1	**2**	**3**	**4**	**5**
strongly disagree	disagree	neither agree nor disagree	agree	strongly agree

10. When something bad happens to me, I take it very hard.

1	**2**	**3**	**4**	**5**
strongly disagree	disagree	neither agree nor disagree	agree	strongly agree

11. When necessary, I can stand up for myself.

1	**2**	**3**	**4**	**5**
strongly disagree	disagree	neither agree nor disagree	agree	strongly agree

12. When I look back at my life, I feel bad about the mistakes I have made.

1	**2**	**3**	**4**	**5**
strongly disagree	disagree	neither agree nor disagree	agree	strongly agree

13. I often feel depressed.

1	**2**	**3**	**4**	**5**
strongly disagree	disagree	neither agree nor disagree	agree	strongly agree

14. I am easily discouraged.

1	**2**	**3**	**4**	**5**
strongly disagree	disagree	neither agree nor disagree	agree	strongly agree

15. I believe life has meaning.

1	2	3	4	5
strongly disagree	disagree	neither agree nor disagree	agree	strongly agree

16. I have the ability to bounce back from setbacks.

1	2	3	4	5
strongly disagree	disagree	neither agree nor disagree	agree	strongly agree

17. When I need help, I can get it from others.

1	2	3	4	5
strongly disagree	disagree	neither agree nor disagree	agree	strongly agree

18. It is easy for me to see beauty in the world.

1	2	3	4	5
strongly disagree	disagree	neither agree nor disagree	agree	strongly agree

19. I tend to be something of a loner.

1	2	3	4	5
strongly disagree	disagree	neither agree nor disagree	agree	strongly agree

20. I often feel happy.

1	2	3	4	5
strongly disagree	disagree	neither agree nor disagree	agree	strongly agree

+ scoring

The first step is to reverse score items 4, 6, 10, 12, 13, 14, and 19. For these items, if you circled 5, change it to a 1, a 4 becomes a 2, a 3 remains a 3, a 2 becomes a 4, and a 1 becomes a 5. After you have made these changes, add your points together for your total score on the Resiliency Test. High scores indicate a high degree of resiliency.

RESILIENCY SCORE	PERCENTILE
80	**85**
74	70
68	**50**
62	30
56	**15**

+ about the resiliency test

The concept of resiliency became of interest to a number of researchers during the 1970s. It was noted that many children living in horrific situations who seemed likely to develop serious problems actually turned out quite well. Children who had an alcoholic father or a schizophrenic mother, children who lived in grinding poverty where drugs were always available, and children who suffered profound neglect both emotionally and physically were not necessarily doomed. Some of them thrived, becoming lawyers, physicians, scientists, writers, or artists. These resilient children succeeded well beyond what anyone could have expected given their start in life. They gave poignant meaning to Robert Louis Stevenson's words, "Life is not a matter of holding good cards but playing a poor hand well."

University of Michigan psychologist Susan Nolen-Hoeksema and her colleagues have spent the past several years studying a similar phenomenon. They were interested in the reactions of people who experienced an unexpected loss or tragedy—the death of a child or an incapacitating injury, for instance. While many people never recover from such trauma, a surprising number not only adjust but experience personal growth. These resilient people typically progress through two stages. First, they must make sense of the tragedy. Ironically, a common strategy for making sense of tragedy is to conclude that it makes no sense. People who took this approach believed in a just world before their loss, meaning that they believed good things happen to good people, bad things happen only to bad people. Following their tragedy, they found the idea that the world is chaotic and unpredictable to be a comforting notion. A second common strategy was to invoke divine intervention, thinking that it was God's will. It is interesting that Nolen-Hoeksema found it was important for people to make sense of their loss within six months if they were to feel better. Those who took longer than six months to come to some understanding did not experience a reduction in their emotional distress.

The second stage experienced by resilient people was discovering some benefit in their loss. Three particular benefits were especially common: a growth in character; increased perspective; and stronger, more meaningful relationships. Nolen-Hoeksema quoted one woman who lost her mother to cancer and who described her subsequent growth with eloquence: "I learned about compassion. I learned about suffering. Suffering leads to compassion. Compassion leads to beauty. It was an opportunity to look at myself and to be non-complacent. I was always very complacent before. I thought I had it made. I was stagnating. It opened my heart, my mind, and my spirit. I wish it had happened another way, but that's the way it happened."

Perhaps one of the more important studies dealing with resiliency was the product of an unhappy serendipity. Along with her colleagues at the University of Michigan, Barbara Fredrickson conducted an investigation of positive emotions, including resiliency, during the spring and summer of 2001. Following the national tragedy of September 11, 2001, these researchers contacted the men and women who had participated in the study and invited them to return for a follow-up interview regarding their reactions to the attacks on the World Trade Center and the Pentagon. This research not only led to a more complete understanding of resilience but also suggested strategies for helping people increase their level of resilience. Let me briefly summarize the findings.

First, resilience appears to be one part of a constellation of traits. While there are always exceptions, resilient people tend to be high in extroversion, emotional stability, and intellectual openness. Second, resilient people experience high levels of optimism, tranquility, and satisfaction with their lives. Third, these people, like those in Nolen-Hoeksema's research, were able to find positive meaning in the problems they experienced following the attacks. And fourth, resilient people were less depressed and experienced fewer negative emotions generally than their nonresilient peers, and they experienced positive emotions more frequently.

One should not assume that everything was rosy with these resilient people; they did experience the same intense anguish, horror, and fear that most Americans felt. But after the crisis they were able to bounce back even stronger than before. At their post-9/11 follow-up interview, resilient people were even more optimistic, tranquil, and satisfied with their lives than they had been earlier that summer. They talked about their blessings, their newfound love for family and friends, and their increased openness in expressing it. They were deeply moved by the events of 9/11 but believed the crisis had helped them grow and be better people than they had been before. In short, they were resilient.

Fredrickson and her colleagues concluded that positive emotions are the most important component of resiliency (I discuss positive mood states in Chapter 14), but this knowledge is of relatively little use because it is nearly impossible for us to conjure positive emotions on command, even when we know it is in our best interest to do so. So the obvious question becomes how to cultivate positive emotions, especially during times of crisis.

The authors suggest that the most effective strategy may be to find positive meaning in tragic events or, during more mundane times, even in ordinary events. Many people find this meaning in their religion or their spiritual beliefs but a common way in which resilient people do this is by gaining a fresh appreciation for the bonds they have with family and friends. After 9/11, one of my students said it well:

> I didn't think anything bad could happen to me but that day showed me how wrong I was. I have friends whose relatives who worked in the World Trade Center—fortunately all of them were okay—but it made me think about the possibility that I could lose someone in my family or even that I could have been killed. For the first time I can remember, I felt a strong sense of gratitude for everything my parents and family have done for me. A couple of days after 9/11, I called my parents to tell them how much I loved them—something I hadn't done in years. Also, I seem to

appreciate even ordinary things more than I did before—little things like spending time with friends or listening to a beautiful song. I really don't think I will ever take life for granted again.

There is a common theme that runs through the research dealing with resiliency, although none of the authors makes it explicit. Resilient people are connected with others, and during difficult and stressful times, they learn to appreciate and value this connection. For those of you who received a low score on the resiliency test and if you tend to be a loner, engage your family and expand your circle of friends and acquaintances. If you already have family and friends, try to change your perspective on what your relationship with them means. Your happiness depends on it.

activities

+ + +

are you an active person?

The following phrases describe people's behaviors, attitudes, and feelings. Indicate the extent to which you agree that the statement describes you.

1. I have more free time than I would like.

1	2	3	4	5
strongly disagree	disagree	neither agree nor disagree	agree	strongly agree

2. I have many activities that are interesting to me.

1	2	3	4	5
strongly disagree	disagree	neither agree nor disagree	agree	strongly agree

3. I spend most of my evenings relaxing—for example, reading or watching television.

1	2	3	4	5
strongly disagree	disagree	neither agree nor disagree	agree	strongly agree

4. I have a full social life.

1	2	3	4	5
strongly disagree	disagree	neither agree nor disagree	agree	strongly agree

5. I am often bored because I have nothing to do.

1	2	3	4	5
strongly disagree	disagree	neither agree nor disagree	agree	strongly agree

6. I am busy from the moment I wake up until the moment I fall asleep.

1	2	3	4	5
strongly disagree	disagree	neither agree nor disagree	agree	strongly agree

7. I do not get enough sleep because I have too much to do.

1	2	3	4	5
strongly disagree	disagree	neither agree nor disagree	agree	strongly agree

8. It is difficult for me to keep busy on weekends.

1	2	3	4	5
strongly disagree	disagree	neither agree nor disagree	agree	strongly agree

9. I look forward to weekends because I have enjoyable activities planned.

1	2	3	4	5
strongly disagree	disagree	neither agree nor disagree	agree	strongly agree

10. I am a couch potato.

1	2	3	4	5
strongly disagree	disagree	neither agree nor disagree	agree	strongly agree

11. I exercise several times per week.

1	2	3	4	5
strongly disagree	disagree	neither agree nor disagree	agree	strongly agree

12. My daily routine involves regular physical exertion.

1	2	3	4	5
strongly disagree	disagree	neither agree nor disagree	agree	strongly agree

13. I try to maintain my cardiovascular endurance.

1	2	3	4	5
strongly disagree	disagree	neither agree nor disagree	agree	strongly agree

14. I can walk briskly for twenty to thirty minutes without tiring.

1	2	3	4	5
strongly disagree	disagree	neither agree nor disagree	agree	strongly agree

15. I exercise regularly to increase my flexibility.

1	2	3	4	5
strongly disagree	disagree	neither agree nor disagree	agree	strongly agree

+ scoring

The first step is to reverse score items 1, 3, 5, 8, and 10. For these items, if you circled 5, change it to a 1, a 4 becomes a 2, a 3 remains a 3, a 2 becomes a 4, and a 1 becomes a 5.

This test consists of two scales, a Busyness Scale and a Physical Activity Scale. To find your Busyness score, add your points for items 1–10. To find your Physical Activity score, add your points for items 11–15. High scores indicate a high degree of busyness and physical activity.

BUSYNESS SCORE	PHYSICAL ACTIVITY SCORE	PERCENTILE
40	18	85
36	15	70
32	12	50
28	9	30
24	6	15

+ about the activity tests

As you can tell from your scores, this test includes two scales: Busyness and Physical Activity, and low scores on either may reflect obstacles to your happiness.

I feel confident that those of you who do not get enough exercise did not need to see a low score on the Physical Activity Test to make you aware of this. If you are like me (I am embarrassed to tell you how low my score was) you know all too well that you should change your sedentary ways. And if you are like me, you may rationalize a bit. After all, I do pass up a cart in favor of walking when I play golf, and I do use the stairs rather than the elevator at my office, but in my heart I know it won't be long before I have to face the consequences of my inability to sustain a regular and vigorous program of exercise.

We all know that exercise is critical to our health. We have seen countless articles about the convincing evidence that exercise reduces the risk of heart disease, which is the leading cause of death. And many of us may be aware that current research suggests that exercise may reduce the likelihood of strokes and some forms of cancer and diabetes. Exercise is also important for maintaining healthy joints, and it can help control pain for those who have developed osteoarthritis. For those of you who tell yourself that you will start a regular program of exercise when you get a little older (again, I plead guilty), it is important to know that many of the protective effects of exercise apply to the young as well as the elderly. Furthermore, vigorous exercise early in life can serve to build stronger bone mass that can reduce the chances of developing osteoporosis during one's later years. The time to start exercising is now.

In recent years a great deal of evidence has been collected to demonstrate that regular exercise also benefits our mental health.

We know, for instance, that exercise is an effective treatment for both anxiety and depression. In an especially important study, Michael Babyak and his colleagues at the Duke University Medical Center found that for older adults suffering from major depression, brisk walking or jogging three times per week was as effective as taking antidepressant medication. And those who exercised were more likely to maintain their improved moods ten months after the study was ended.

The psychological benefits of exercise are not limited to those who are suffering from clinical anxiety or depression. In one study of typical women, it was found that the women's moods were significantly more positive after as little as ten minutes of vigorous physical exercise. Those women who felt the worst before the exercise benefited the most.

As we get older, exercise may become even more important to our mental health. A series of recent studies have demonstrated that exercise can help maintain our intellectual sharpness. It can increase our verbal fluency, our memory, and our ability to plan ahead. Needless to say, our happiness and our satisfaction with our lives will certainly be enhanced if we retain our ability to use our minds as we age.

Professionals who specialize in this area are perplexed as to why so few people take this message seriously. Researchers point out that the surgeon general's 1964 report on smoking and health had a profound effect on the behavior of Americans, but over the thirty years since professional organizations began to issue guidelines about physical activity, the percentage of people who exercise regularly has actually declined. This distressing finding has inspired hundreds of additional studies that have searched for effective strategies to help both children and adults increase their levels of physical activity. Some of these projects have used very creative strategies, but most of them seem to have several elements in common, elements that reflect advice that you probably have heard before. First, select physical activities that you enjoy. If you find jogging to be both painful and boring (as I do), you will never stick with it long enough to benefit from it, much less to reach that mystical (I suspect *mythical* is a better word) endorphin high that joggers are always talking about. Swimming, bowling, gardening, dancing, aerobics, and even simple walking are all activities that have both medical and psychological benefits.

Second, join a group. Not only will this make the experience more enjoyable by combining social activity with the physical, but it will serve as an important source of motivation. It is all too easy to pass on a visit to the gym if you go by yourself, but it is a little more difficult to skip an aerobics class if you know that your friends are expecting you. Social pressure can keep you going during those inevitable slumps in your motivation.

Third, find someone—a spouse, a friend, a colleague—to nag you about it. Although the researchers who did these studies did not use the term *nag*, that is essentially what many of them did. They used both personal and computerized telephone calls and mass mailings to remind people about their commitment and to inquire about their progress. And it worked. I suspect most of us who find it difficult to keep our promises to ourselves to exercise feel guilty when we break them, so a little nagging can work wonders. By the way, I do intend to practice what I preach so ask me in a year how I am doing. I feel confident I will have more strength and endurance and greater flexibility. I hope you will too.

Now let me say a few words about busyness. Busyness is not a topic that has received much research attention, but I have been impressed over the years by the number of unhappy clients I have seen who have so little to do. These people go to work, come home and put a frozen dinner in the oven, and spend the rest of the evening hypnotized by the flicker from their television screen. I do not recall meeting a single happy person who was not able to fill his or her time fairly completely. It is not always the case that all of these activities are fun, or even enjoyable. Many of these people work hard, have numerous family obligations, and then fill up their evenings with various community obligations. But they are busy, and they do see their activities as important and meaningful. If you received a low score on the Busyness Test, you owe it to yourself to find more ways to fill your time and to fill it with meaningful activities. And if you had a low score on the Physical Activity Test, as I suspect you did, a good place to start would be to join a group that will motivate you to exercise regularly.

One final thought. I do believe it is possible to be too busy. I have also seen clients who do not know what it feels like to be without stress. These people take on more obligations than they can possibly meet, and it is not unusual for them to sacrifice sleep time in a futile effort to get everything done. I am not one of those psychologists who believes we should always place ourselves first, but I do believe that we owe it to ourselves to strive for a balance that allows us to find satisfaction and happiness in our day-to-day lives.

+ 21 +

how interested are you in the world around you?

The following phrases describe people's behaviors, attitudes, and feelings. Indicate the extent to which you agree that the statement describes you.

1. When Mars passed close to Earth, I was eager to see it.

1 strongly disagree	2 disagree	3 neither agree nor disagree	4 agree	5 strongly agree

2. I would like to know more about how the world works.

1 strongly disagree	2 disagree	3 neither agree nor disagree	4 agree	5 strongly agree

3. I enjoy television shows about strange and exotic animals.

1	2	3	4	5
strongly disagree	disagree	neither agree nor disagree	agree	strongly agree

4. I wish I knew if life existed on other planets.

1	2	3	4	5
strongly disagree	disagree	neither agree nor disagree	agree	strongly agree

5. I enjoy learning about the customs of people from other countries.

1	2	3	4	5
strongly disagree	disagree	neither agree nor disagree	agree	strongly agree

6. Watching the History or Discovery channels is a waste of time.

1	2	3	4	5
strongly disagree	disagree	neither agree nor disagree	agree	strongly agree

7. When I was a child I was fascinated by dinosaurs.

1	2	3	4	5
strongly disagree	disagree	neither agree nor disagree	agree	strongly agree

8. I often wonder why people do the things they do.

1	2	3	4	5
strongly disagree	disagree	neither agree nor disagree	agree	strongly agree

9. Once you are an adult, it is a waste of time to learn anything new.

1	2	3	4	5
strongly disagree	disagree	neither agree nor disagree	agree	strongly agree

10. I enjoy reading articles about medical discoveries.

1	2	3	4	5
strongly disagree	disagree	neither agree nor disagree	agree	strongly agree

11. I get a feeling of satisfaction from solving a difficult problem.

1	2	3	4	5
strongly disagree	disagree	neither agree nor disagree	agree	strongly agree

12. I enjoy games that make you think.

1	2	3	4	5
strongly disagree	disagree	neither agree nor disagree	agree	strongly agree

13. I enjoy learning about how people lived thousands of years ago.

1	2	3	4	5
strongly disagree	disagree	neither agree nor disagree	agree	strongly agree

14. I have great admiration for creative people.

1	2	3	4	5
strongly disagree	disagree	neither agree nor disagree	agree	strongly agree

15. I do not have enough time to pursue all my interests.

1	2	3	4	5
strongly disagree	disagree	neither agree nor disagree	agree	strongly agree

16. I would rather be entertained than educated.

1	2	3	4	5
strongly disagree	disagree	neither agree nor disagree	agree	strongly agree

+ scoring

The first step is to reverse score items 6, 9, and 16. For these items, if you circled 5, change it to a 1, a 4 becomes a 2, a 3 remains a 3, a 2 becomes a 4, and a 1 becomes a 5. After you have made these changes, add your points together for your total score on the Interest Test. High scores indicate a high degree of interest in the world around you.

INTEREST SCORE	PERCENTILE
63	**85**
58	70
52	**50**
46	30
41	**15**

+ about the interest test

What do you suppose was the single most popular Internet event ever?

I have to admit that my thoughts were way off the mark. My first guess was that it had something to do with a passionate moment between two celebrities caught on tape or a history-making sports event. According to *Discover Magazine,* it was the photos of Mars that were transmitted back to Earth by the *Pathfinder* spacecraft. This online photo display received 566 million hits. Even the most shocking Hollywood scandal does not come close to being this popular.

Psychologist Michael Schulman argued that the incredible interest generated by the Mars photos is significant because it illustrates that human behavior is motivated by curiosity, a straightforward desire to know things. This is remarkable because most psychological theories are based on the assumption that human behavior is motivated by the desire to satisfy some basic drive, such as hunger or sex. But the interest in Mars may illustrate that we have a need to know things simply because they are interesting. Schulman's point nicely distinguishes positive psychology from the more traditional views. While traditional theorists view people as a bundle of basic needs that we are driven to satisfy and define mental health as simply the absence of pathology, Schulman believes that we are capable of so much more. We are born with an interest in the world around us and we have an innate desire to learn everything we can about how it works.

We can see this readily in our children. Like most parents, I discovered that my two boys had more questions than I had answers. What is the name of that animal? Where does the sun go at night? Is this story real? The questions were endless. Schulman contends that the questions will continue to be endless so long as children are not punished or mocked for their curiosity or if they do not come to associate learning with mind-numbing exercises that are all too often a part of school curricula. If our children's interest in the world is to survive to adulthood, it must be nourished and encouraged.

Interest can take a variety of forms, according to Schulman. He proposed six basic categories. People with inventive interests might try to develop an a more energy-efficient light bulb or a new, tastier recipe for lasagna. A person with inductive interests might want to explain electromagnetism or why some people engage in self-destructive behavior. Writing a novel or designing a piece of furniture would reflect imaginative interests, while finding the cause of a patient's heart condition or the tendency of a car to overheat would reflect diagnostic interests. Discovering a strategy to win the war on terrorism or beating your friends at poker would reflect tactical interests, and designing a system that makes it possible for people to share their music over the Internet or plotting the best route for your trip to see the grandparents would reflect symbolic/mathematical interests.

Although I believe we all have interest in several of these areas, few of us are interested in everything, and we should not feel an obligation to be so. I had one child who knew so much about dinosaurs by the time he was five, he could have been a guide at any museum of natural history. The other child had only a passing interest in anything that was not part of the present, but he was compelled to disassemble most every toy he received in an effort to learn how it worked. They both have retained their childhood interests into their adult years, and these interests have served them well. Their interests have not only provided them with a means of earning a living but have helped generate an enthusiasm and excitement about what they do.

I suspect that not many of you received a low score on this scale. Low scorers would not have much interest in any book that offered an opportunity to understand themselves better. But it may be the case that you have failed to capitalize on your natural interest in the world, that your interest has become somewhat dormant. This happened to a friend of mine, whom I'll call Ned. Ned was a supply officer in the navy, and while he did not dislike his job, he did not find it very satisfying. He had a bleak period for several years when the demands of his career and three young children filled his time. But when his children became a little older, he spent much of his weekends on home-improvement projects. To Ned, home improvement was much more than putting a fresh coat of paint on the window frames or cleaning a slow-draining sink. I marveled at his study with its built-in cabinets and bookcases, and his laundry room was the envy of the neighborhood. It was not long before his friends and neighbors were asking him to do similar projects for them, and when he had completed twenty years of service he retired from the navy and began doing home remodeling full time. Ned's success in his second career resulted largely from his strong interest in what he was doing. He was always looking for new products that he could use in his work, and he continued to read trade journals to improve his technique.

While Ned's story is quite exceptional, I do believe it is possible for anyone to find more satisfaction and happiness by making an active effort to pursue his or her interests. The key is to refuse to be satisfied with the status quo. If you enjoy your weekly poker games, read books about strategy, learn more about the odds of drawing to that inside straight, and read about human behavior so you can have a better idea if your bitter rival is bluffing. If you like the *Star Trek* series (Captain Picard is by far my favorite), attend the presentations at your local observatory, look for magazine articles about the possibility of traveling faster than the speed of light, and find the Web sites that provide close-up photos of the planets. Everyone has something they enjoy doing that provides an opportunity to learn more, to satisfy your innate need to know how the world works.

The problem, I think, is that too many of us become complacent and lazy. We are tired at the end of the day and it is all too easy to plop down in our favorite chair and watch the latest reality show. But if we give in to this tendency, we are denying a very basic aspect of our nature, and hence making it very difficult to experience the happiness and joy that can result from stretching our minds and satisfying our need to know. It may take some effort to revive your natural curiosity about the world, but it is an effort that will provide you with great satisfaction.

do you have satisfying hobbies?

The following phrases describe people's behaviors, attitudes, and feelings. Indicate the extent to which you agree that the statement describes you.

1. I have a hobby that I really enjoy.

1	2	3	4	5
strongly disagree	disagree	neither agree nor disagree	agree	strongly agree

2. My hobby requires that I learn new things.

1	2	3	4	5
strongly disagree	disagree	neither agree nor disagree	agree	strongly agree

3. To be good at my hobby requires that I spend time on it or practice.

1	2	3	4	5
strongly disagree	disagree	neither agree nor disagree	agree	strongly agree

4. I look forward to evenings and weekends so I can spend more time on my hobby.

1	2	3	4	5
strongly disagree	disagree	neither agree nor disagree	agree	strongly agree

5. My hobby involves physical activity.

1	2	3	4	5
strongly disagree	disagree	neither agree nor disagree	agree	strongly agree

6. I enjoy talking about my hobby with others.

1	2	3	4	5
strongly disagree	disagree	neither agree nor disagree	agree	strongly agree

7. I often find myself thinking about my hobby.

1	2	3	4	5
strongly disagree	disagree	neither agree nor disagree	agree	strongly agree

8. When engaged with my hobby, I forget about my problems.

1	2	3	4	5
strongly disagree	disagree	neither agree nor disagree	agree	strongly agree

9. My life is richer as a result of my hobby.

1	2	3	4	5
strongly disagree	disagree	neither agree nor disagree	agree	strongly agree

10. My family approves of my hobby.

1	2	3	4	5
strongly disagree	disagree	neither agree nor disagree	agree	strongly agree

11. My hobby keeps me busy.

1	2	3	4	5
strongly disagree	disagree	neither agree nor disagree	agree	strongly agree

12. I have more than one hobby.

1	2	3	4	5
strongly disagree	disagree	neither agree nor disagree	agree	strongly agree

13. My hobby causes conflict with those close to me.

1	2	3	4	5
strongly disagree	disagree	neither agree nor disagree	agree	strongly agree

14. There is a good chance that I will have other hobbies in the coming years.

1	2	3	4	5
strongly disagree	disagree	neither agree nor disagree	agree	strongly agree

15. If I had to give up my hobby, it would not matter much to me.

1	2	3	4	5
strongly disagree	disagree	neither agree nor disagree	agree	strongly agree

16. My hobby requires that I become involved with other people.

1	2	3	4	5
strongly disagree	disagree	neither agree nor disagree	agree	strongly agree

+ scoring

The first step is to reverse score items 13 and 15. For these items, if you circled 5, change it to a 1, a 4 becomes a 2, a 3 remains a 3, a 2 becomes a 4, and a 1 becomes a 5. After you have made these changes, add your points together for your total score on the Hobby Satisfaction Test. High scores indicate a high degree of happiness with your hobby.

HOBBY SATISFACTION SCORE	PERCENTILE
54	85
49	70
44	50
39	30
34	15

+ about the hobby satisfaction test

Most of the happy people I have known have been passionate about a hobby. These people are busy, active, and involved. They are excited about the world around them and never tire of learning more about it. While some happy people may be able to satisfy their need for an active, challenging, and involved life through their work alone, a majority fill their few precious extra hours by pursuing a hobby.

Let me be clear about one thing. Not everything one likes to do in his or her spare time qualifies as a hobby. Prowling shopping malls day after day and watching every televised sporting event are not hobbies. They may be ways to pass the time, rather empty ways to my mind, but they are not hobbies. To qualify as a hobby, an activity must meet one of three criteria, and the most satisfying hobbies meet two, and often all three, of them. The first of these requirements is that your hobby stretches your mind, it inspires you to learn something new. Most collectors have this need to learn. I had a friend who, as a child, received a set of cardboard templates for displaying U.S. coins of the past hundred years. It took him several years to fill his display cards and fifteen years later he was collecting very old coins from around the world. Although his field was electrical engineering, he had become quite knowledgeable about the politics and economics of a variety of societies throughout history. Most any type of collection, whether it is stamps, art, or even baseball cards, requires that people expand their knowledge, to learn more about the world in which they live. Another excellent example of this first hobby category can be found in a colleague of mine at the university. He is a chemistry professor, and perhaps because of his academic background, he became interested in wine (although I must point out that drinking in itself does not qualify as a hobby). He learned so much about his hobby that currently he offers noncredit classes to the community, something he finds immensely satisfying.

The second criteria to qualify an activity as a hobby is that it involves physical activity. The importance of physical activity comes up in several chapters but in short, there is clear and convincing evidence that physical activity promotes both medical and psychological health. The obvious examples of hobbies that meet this criteria are those involving sports. I have a number of friends who meet during lunch hour for pick-up basketball games or play tennis or softball. For those who are not inclined toward sports, gardening or woodworking are wonderful hobbies that not only demand physical activity but can add a little beauty to your world as well. The line between a hobby and exercise can become a little blurry (and it may not be very important anyway), but hobbies are enjoyable activities, not something you have to force yourself to do. So dedicated joggers, in my view, are exercising, not pursuing a hobby. Despite their protestations, I simply do not believe that anyone would jog purely for the joy of the activity if it did not have health benefits.

The third criteria is that a hobby may involve social contact. An example that seemed to be more popular a few years ago before the Internet bubble burst than it is now is investment clubs. The people I knew who belong to these groups were, of course, interested in increasing their net worth, but it seemed to me that their monthly meetings where they could share information about what they had learned were the focus of their experience. Book clubs, chess clubs, and most volunteer activities are all examples of this type of hobby—activities in which the primary benefit is social interaction. This is another topic that is discussed in several chapters: happy people have numerous and rewarding social interactions.

As I mentioned earlier, most hobbies, and certainly the best ones, meet two or even three of these criteria. My father enjoyed a hobby for many years that provides a good example. He was a carpenter and I am not sure how he ever came to develop his particular passion, but he grew roses. It began with a couple of rose bushes along the back fence, which quickly became a row of plants. And before five years passed, the lawn was completely replaced with beds for the roses. He would spend an hour each morning before going to work tending to his 150 bushes and another hour each evening. Later on during the evening he read about flowers and became an expert on both the history and the cultivation of roses, and over the years he developed his own hybrids. It was not long before he began entering his flowers in the local rose shows, and he almost always came home with a fistful of blue ribbons. His skill and acumen did not go unnoticed, and he served as an officer in the Denver Rose Society for a number of years. It was the perfect hobby for my dad. There was the obvious physical activity in tending to his plants, but it also motivated him to stretch his mind and his social contacts. He is an intelligent man but, given his working-class background, he was not accustomed to extensive reading. And he was not naturally a gregarious person, so his involvement with the Rose Society provided him with social interactions he would not otherwise have had. I know that his hobby greatly enriched his life and increased his happiness.

As a second example, I want to talk about the perfect hobby—mine, of course—namely, golf. I try to play a couple of times each week, and because I walk, it provides me with much-needed physical activity. Not only have I learned a great deal about the history of the sport but I have also learned a little about physics in trying to understand the mechanics of the game and quite a bit about statistics during endless discussions with friends about the handicapping system. And the social contacts are a very important part of the experience. My friends and I talk as we walk the course, and then, of course, there is the proverbial nineteenth hole at the end of every round. I am being perhaps more than a little facetious when I say that golf is the perfect hobby, but it has been a great solace for me during some difficult times. It is the perfect hobby for me because it engages me, so it allows me to forget my problems, even if only for a few hours. As was the case with my dad and his roses, golf has enriched my life and helped me be a happier person.

If you received a low score on this scale and you are not happy, it would be worth your while to develop a hobby. There has been very little research regarding the link between having a hobby and happiness, but we do know that encouraging the elderly to develop hobbies does result in increased happiness. So the odds are good that it would do the same for you, even if you are younger. If you do not know where to begin, start with your friends. What do they like to do? What are their hobbies? If any of these activities interest you, it would be easy to get started with your friends' help. A second strategy is to take a course or two through your local adult education or recreational facility. Virginia Beach, the city in which I live, is a rather small town, but they offer several dozen courses every season that reflect a wide variety of interests. Finally, simply decide what really interests you and begin to learn more about it. A colleague loved cowboy movies and his interest led to his becoming an active member of a club that dresses in the clothing of the old west and has shooting competitions, a hobby that I did not know existed until my friend told me about it. The key is to follow your interests. If you do, you will find your life expanding as you become more involved with the world around you.

how much do you care about others?

The following phrases describe people's behaviors, attitudes, and feelings. Indicate the extent to which you agree that the statement describes you.

1. I try hard to make others feel welcome when they visit me.

1	2	3	4	5
strongly disagree	disagree	neither agree nor disagree	agree	strongly agree

2. I seldom take time for other people.

1	2	3	4	5
strongly disagree	disagree	neither agree nor disagree	agree	strongly agree

3. I try to anticipate the needs of others.

1 strongly disagree	**2** disagree	**3** neither agree nor disagree	**4** agree	**5** strongly agree

4. Finishing my own work is much more important than helping others with theirs.

1 strongly disagree	**2** disagree	**3** neither agree nor disagree	**4** agree	**5** strongly agree

5. It makes me feel wonderful to help others.

1 strongly disagree	**2** disagree	**3** neither agree nor disagree	**4** agree	**5** strongly agree

6. I am concerned about my friends and relatives.

1 strongly disagree	**2** disagree	**3** neither agree nor disagree	**4** agree	**5** strongly agree

7. I can think of something good to say about most everyone I know.

1 strongly disagree	**2** disagree	**3** neither agree nor disagree	**4** agree	**5** strongly agree

8. I tend to feel superior to others.

1 strongly disagree	**2** disagree	**3** neither agree nor disagree	**4** agree	**5** strongly agree

9. I do not care about the feelings of others.

1	2	3	4	5
strongly disagree	disagree	neither agree nor disagree	agree	strongly agree

10. I sometimes make others feel uncomfortable.

1	2	3	4	5
strongly disagree	disagree	neither agree nor disagree	agree	strongly agree

11. It does not bother me to see people less fortunate than I who are begging for money.

1	2	3	4	5
strongly disagree	disagree	neither agree nor disagree	agree	strongly agree

12. When I hear stories about people who have suffered some misfortune, I want to help.

1	2	3	4	5
strongly disagree	disagree	neither agree nor disagree	agree	strongly agree

13. I make anonymous contributions to charities.

1	2	3	4	5
strongly disagree	disagree	neither agree nor disagree	agree	strongly agree

14. I feel sad when I read articles about people elsewhere in the world who are suffering.

1	2	3	4	5
strongly disagree	disagree	neither agree nor disagree	agree	strongly agree

15. I would enjoy spending time doing volunteer work for those less fortunate than myself.

1	2	3	4	5
strongly disagree	disagree	neither agree nor disagree	agree	strongly agree

+ scoring

The first step is to reverse score items 2, 4, 8, 9, 10, and 11. For these items, if you circled 5, change it to a 1, a 4 becomes a 2, a 3 remains a 3, a 2 becomes a 4, and a 1 becomes a 5. After you have made these changes, add your points together for your total score on the Altruism Test. High scores indicate a high degree of altruism.

ALTRUISM SCORE	PERCENTILE
56	**85**
52	70
47	**50**
42	30
37	**15**

+ about the altruism test

Perhaps no other single characteristic can contribute as much to our happiness as can altruism. Psychologist Martin Seligman, one of the leaders of the positive psychology movement, cited the following aphorism in his book *Authentic Happiness:*

If you want to be happy . . .
  for an hour, take a nap.
  for a day, go fishing.
  for a month, get married.
  for a year, get an inheritance.
  for a lifetime, help someone.

Happy people are involved with other people. They care about how others feel and are willing to do what they can to relieve their suffering and their distress. They share both the joy and the despair experienced by people they have never met, as well as those they know well. They are truly a full-fledged member of the human race.

Because the positive psychology movement is so new, we are just beginning to learn about the relationship between altruism and life satisfaction, but researchers have been studying altruism for several decades now. One finding resulting from this research is that there is a strong link between altruism and another emotion, empathy. Empathy can be thought of as a vicarious emotional response. It reflects our ability to share the emotional experiences of others. Highly empathic people regularly have the experience of their eyes filling with tears when they see a segment on the news about hungry children or people who have become disabled in an accident. Empathic people also share in the joy of an athlete who sets a new school record or a child who has performed well at a recital. These people share the emotional experiences of others, even when the others are strangers.

Empathy is the emotion that triggers altruism. This empathy-altruism link has been thoroughly explored by psychologist C. Daniel Batson of the University of Kansas. With the help of his colleagues, Batson has shown that empathic people will consistently pass up opportunities for self-gain to help others. And in response to his cynical critics who argue that altruism is motivated by some subtle form of selfishness, such as to help one feel good about one's self or to win the approval of others, Batson has shown that people are indeed capable of behaving in a truly selfless way. In his research he found that altruistic behavior did not result from a desire to avoid disapproval, shame, or guilt, nor was it motivated by a desire to feel good about one's self or to enhance one's reputation. Many people clearly have the capacity to perform purely selfless acts.

Most of us probably engage in small acts of altruism every day. We give a friend a ride even when it is inconvenient, we share our notes with a classmate even though it could affect the grading curve, or we help an elderly person pick up a dropped package even though our own back is not feeling all that great. Researchers have identified several other examples of altruism that you may never have considered. In one interesting example, Harry Prapavessis and Albert Carron of the University of Auckland in New Zealand examined the altruistic behavior of high-level cricket players. These athletes were playing in a league from which players for the national team would be selected, and so they had conflicting interests. They wanted their team to do well but they also wanted to stand out as individual athletes to increase the odds that they would be selected to represent their country. The researchers found that most of the athletes indicated that they did make personal sacrifices for the good of the team, including putting aside their personal goals if they conflicted with the team's goals. Furthermore, this willingness to make personal sacrifices was related to team cohesiveness, something that every coach wants his or her team to achieve. We tend to think of high-level athletes as egotistical and self-centered (and I'm sure many of them are), but they are clearly capable of altruism for the good of the team.

A second very interesting example of altruism was provided in psychologists Bella DePaulo and Deborah Kasby's research about lying. Their finding that most people tell lies often and regularly shocked many people, but this widespread failure to tell the truth may not be as bad as it sounds at first blush. First, a very small percentage of the lies were mean spirited, the sort of lies that might be intended to hurt or embarrass an acquaintance. Many of the lies were motivated by a sense of self-protection. The college student, for instance, who tells his father that he has been studying hard or the person who tells an acquaintance that he or she is not dating anyone to protect personal privacy. A substantial percentage of the lies told were classified as altruistic lies. The person who tells his spouse that she does not look overweight in the new dress or the person who declines a friend's invitation to a movie with the excuse of family obligations because she has already made plans with another friend. This type of lie was surprisingly common. Spouses reported that they lied to their partner once in every ten interactions, and people in romantic relationships lied once in every three encounters. The researchers concluded that these altruistic lies serve to convey caring and concern by protecting the partner's feelings and self-esteem. Most of us seem to believe that honesty is not always the best policy.

Because research in this area is so new, no one has yet developed therapies specifically to increase one's altruism, though advice columnists have known for decades the value of altruism in increasing life satisfaction. Fifty years ago, Ann Landers was recommending that people mired in misery and self-pity get involved with some sort of volunteer work. I think her advice is still great today, but I also believe that you can increase your happiness by being altruistic in small ways. When your spouse or roommate asks for your help while you are watching your favorite television show, turn off the set and help. A week later you would have forgotten the show anyway, but your kindness and selflessness will strengthen your relationship and this is likely to pay rich dividends. When a child appears at your door selling raffle tickets for the school library, spend a few minutes talking to the child. Even if you do not want to spend the money for a ticket you could make a small contribution and offer encouragement. The child will leave with a good feeling and that gives you the right to feel good as well. If you have the time, follow Ann Landers's advice and get involved in a structured volunteer activity. Read to the sick and elderly, build a house for humanity, serve as a scoutmaster. It will enrich your life.

I recognize the paradox here. I am suggesting that you engage in an altruistic activity so you will feel better. This distorts the meaning of altruism, but if you are unhappy, if you feel that your life lacks meaning, being altruistic for selfish reasons is a place to start. I predict that if you make a habit of your newfound altruism, it will not be long before you forget all about the benefits you are getting out of the deal. You will begin to focus on the people you are helping; and once you do that, you are well on your way to becoming a happier person.

does your life have meaning?

The following phrases describe people's behaviors, attitudes, and feelings. Indicate the extent to which you agree that the statement describes you.

1. I often feel that my life has no purpose.

1	2	3	4	5
strongly disagree	disagree	neither agree nor disagree	agree	strongly agree

2. I have much to look forward to.

1	2	3	4	5
strongly disagree	disagree	neither agree nor disagree	agree	strongly agree

3. I feel bored much of the time.

1	2	3	4	5
strongly disagree	disagree	neither agree nor disagree	agree	strongly agree

4. I feel good about what I have done with my life.

1	2	3	4	5
strongly disagree	disagree	neither agree nor disagree	agree	strongly agree

5. If I were to die tomorrow, it would not really matter to anyone.

1	2	3	4	5
strongly disagree	disagree	neither agree nor disagree	agree	strongly agree

6. The biggest challenge in life is filling the time.

1	2	3	4	5
strongly disagree	disagree	neither agree nor disagree	agree	strongly agree

7. Life is inherently meaningless.

1	2	3	4	5
strongly disagree	disagree	neither agree nor disagree	agree	strongly agree

8. I often feel excited by the challenges that I face.

1	2	3	4	5
strongly disagree	disagree	neither agree nor disagree	agree	strongly agree

9. I have trouble finding anything to do that I enjoy.

1	2	3	4	5
strongly disagree	disagree	neither agree nor disagree	agree	strongly agree

10. I have very strong feelings about some issues.

1	2	3	4	5
strongly disagree	disagree	neither agree nor disagree	agree	strongly agree

11. In my own small way, I believe I am making the world a better place.

1	2	3	4	5
strongly disagree	disagree	neither agree nor disagree	agree	strongly agree

12. I have a clear set of goals.

1	2	3	4	5
strongly disagree	disagree	neither agree nor disagree	agree	strongly agree

13. There are people who count on me.

1	2	3	4	5
strongly disagree	disagree	neither agree nor disagree	agree	strongly agree

14. The work I do is pretty useless.

1	2	3	4	5
strongly disagree	disagree	neither agree nor disagree	agree	strongly agree

15. I have a strong reaction to certain events in the news.

1	2	3	4	5
strongly disagree	disagree	neither agree nor disagree	agree	strongly agree

16. Most people I know lead rather empty lives.

1	2	3	4	5
strongly disagree	disagree	neither agree nor disagree	agree	strongly agree

17. There is not much that I really care about.

1	2	3	4	5
strongly disagree	disagree	neither agree nor disagree	agree	strongly agree

18. One person can make a difference in the world.

1	2	3	4	5
strongly disagree	disagree	neither agree nor disagree	agree	strongly agree

+ scoring

The first step is to reverse score items 1, 3, 5, 6, 7, 9, 14, 16, and 17. For these items, if you circled 5, change it to a 1, a 4 becomes a 2, a 3 remains a 3, a 2 becomes a 4, and a 1 becomes a 5. After you have made these changes, add your points together for your total score on the Meaningfulness Test. High scores indicate a high degree of meaningfulness.

MEANINGFULNESS SCORE	PERCENTILE
72	**85**
67	70
61	**50**
55	30
50	**15**

+ about the meaningfulness test

At birth, we humans are little more than a bundle of biological drives. We demand to have our hunger satisfied and our thirst quenched. We expect to be safe, comfortable, and warm. And then, after a little more than a decade passes, we feel compelled to satisfy our need to reproduce. Perhaps there was a time in human history when people were content as long as they managed to satisfy these needs, but it is likely that very early on humans wanted more, they wanted their lives to be meaningful.

We humans are capable of understanding that we have a future and that in this future looms our death. Anthropologists tell us that before recorded history, spiritual leaders, philosophers, and artists were trying to make sense of our transition from birth to death, to find the meaning of life, and they continue to do so. But it has only been in recent years, with the emergence of positive psychology, that research psychologists have addressed this issue.

Case Western Reserve psychologist, Roy Baumeister, one of the most prominent of these theorists, has suggested that there are four levels of meaning that we strive to satisfy. Our need for purpose is first. We yearn to find a connection between the present and the future. One way that we can do this is to have goals, to publish a novel or to become manager of our department at work. While many people find their purpose in such goals, it seems to me that this can be a dangerous approach. Many of us will fail to accomplish the often lofty objectives we set for ourselves in our youth, and for many of those who do make it to their personal summit, they are left wondering what the point of it all was. Although I believe it is crucial to have goals, I think a better strategy for finding purpose lies in Baumeister's second suggestion: finding fulfillments. We can find fulfillment in our family, in our friends, and in helping other people. There was a touching story in my local newspaper recently about a man who found fulfillment in feeding more than one hundred feral cats who lived in an abandoned warehouse. Finding our purpose in the context of our relationship with other living creatures is less likely to end in disappointment than finding purpose in achieving status, I think.

The fulfillments we find meaningful will reflect our values. These values can be religious or secular in nature, but it is important for us to have a set of principles to enable us to determine if our behavior is right or wrong, good or bad. Explicit values will serve to guide us, to enable us to make decisions that will reduce our feelings of guilt, anxiety, regret, or despair and to increase our feelings of joy, satisfaction, and meaningfulness. People who base their lives on expediency are unlikely to find much meaning in them.

A sense of self-efficacy is a third way of finding meaning. We must have the belief that we have the ability to achieve our purpose and live in accord with our values if they are to mean anything.

And fourth, we must have a strong sense of self-esteem. Self-esteem has been the focus of thousands of research studies and has been shown to be related to a wide variety of life experiences. The evidence is clear that without a healthy sense of self-worth, we are unlikely to find life either meaningful or satisfying. It is important to keep in mind that self-esteem does not necessarily come from individual accomplishment. It can, but it can also be derived from being a member of a group that is perceived to be worthwhile. Simply being a kind and responsible member of one's community is more than enough justification for one to feel good about himself or herself.

Baumeister reports that people who have satisfied all four of these needs are likely to find their lives highly meaningful, whereas those who are not able to satisfy at least one are likely to experience their lives as rather empty. That there are four ways in which we can find meaning is reassuring, as there are bound to be times in our lives during which we fall short in one area or another. If we experience divorce, we can continue to find meaning in working toward our goals. If we are laid off our job, we can focus on the fulfillment offered by having a loving relationship with our family.

The benefits of finding meaning in our lives have been well documented. Such people have fewer physical illnesses and visit their physicians less often. They are less likely to experience despair, and they have more positive mood states. They even get better grades in college.

While experiencing life as meaningful appears to be a necessary condition for happiness, it is not sufficient. There are undoubtedly many people who have extremely meaningful but unhappy lives. Terrorists, for example, undoubtedly find their lives to be meaningful even though it would seem to be impossible for them to be happy. Health professionals who dedicate their lives to treating the severely injured or ill may have meaningful yet unhappy lives. And there are some situations in which it appears that we must knowingly sacrifice happiness for meaningfulness. In Chapter 4, I discussed research that shows that parents with young children experience a decline in their happiness. Perhaps they were surprised that they were less happy after the birth of their first child, but the countless couples who have a second child are knowingly making the decision to sacrifice happiness for meaningfulness.

If you received a low score on the Meaningfulness Test, Baumeister's work does offer suggestions for how you can find more meaning. He has presented evidence that writing about the unhappy events in your life can help you discover a structure to your thoughts, feelings, and behaviors that will enable you to develop new insights and coping strategies. So write a story about an important, distressing event in your life. Include the objective facts, but do not neglect the background and the context in which the unfortunate event occurred. Researchers have found that typical stories begin with a bad event or burden, but they often end in a positive way. The hero of the story (you) usually learns to overcome adversity and develops into a person who is good, moral, and strong.

Nick, after many protestations that it was a silly idea, agreed to write such a story about his divorce, which had left him feeling devastated, lonely, and hopeless. The first half of his story delineated his failures as a husband in excruciating detail, but gradually the story became more positive. His characterization of himself shifted from a self-absorbed, dishonest man to one who wasn't as strong as he should have been. By the end of the story, he had learned from his mistakes and vowed to value and respect all future relationships. Three years later he remarried and he acquired a strong sense of self-efficacy and self-worth by living up to the standards he had set for himself in his story.

You should be warned that although there is compelling evidence that this story-writing approach has clear benefits for both physical and mental health, it is often the case that people feel worse immediately after completing this task. If you decide to try this approach, you may find it painful at the beginning and you may still feel bad even when you finish your narrative with a happy ending. Be patient. The insight and desire to restructure your life takes a little time to develop, but the odds are excellent that it will happen for you.

As I said at the beginning of this book, I hope you found the tests useful in identifying your strengths as well as those areas that could use a little tweaking in order for you to be a happier person. Nothing would please me more than if you found this book to be a useful tool in improving your level of satisfaction with your life.

I wanted to say a few words for those of you who received low scores on many of the scales. You may feel hopeless if your scores indicate that you need to change a dozen or so of your personal qualities in order to be happy, but it is important to keep in mind that the characteristics discussed in this book tend to be interrelated. This means that, even if you received scores at the 15th percentile on half of the tests, you do not necessarily need a complete personality makeover. Suppose, for example, that three of your low scores were on the friends, romantic partner, and sociability tests. It would probably be the case that by increasing your sociability, you would also improve your friendships and increase your odds of finding a suitable romantic partner. Similarly, if you work on increasing your optimism, you will probably experience corresponding increases in your trust, internal control, and your interests. Researchers have yet to unravel all of these interrelationships, but you are probably the best judge of how it will work for you. These quizzes may have helped you articulate your strengths and weaknesses, but you undoubtedly already had a pretty clear idea of what they were. After all, these are self-report scales, and you are the one who did the reporting.

If you feel comfortable doing so, you may find it helpful to discuss the results of your tests with a close friend or family member. We do not always see ourselves as clearly as we might; therefore, a trusted confidant may be able to provide you with additional insights. You might also find it useful to discuss your plans for the changes you want to make in your life with this person. The truth can be painful, so if you ask for advice try not to be hurt by what you hear. Be grateful that you have someone in your life who cares enough to be honest with you.

Change is never easy, but there is ample research that proves it is possible. Once you develop your plan for change, be persistent and do not give up. As long as you keep trying, you are destined to prevail. If you do get stuck, do not hesitate to consult a mental health professional. Even if you think you cannot afford to see one, the odds are excellent that you can find one who will see you for a nominal fee. Most cities of any size have public mental health services, and if there is a university or medical school in your area, they may offer services at no cost or a very modest fee as part of their training mission.

Remember, if you received a very low score on the Happiness Tests in Chapter 1, it is not necessary for you to go through life feeling so miserable. The new breed of positive psychologists have convincingly demonstrated that it is possible for you to enjoy your life more. And as long as you continue your efforts to change, I feel confident that you will succeed.